In the Grip of Grace

MAX LUCADO

In the

Grip of

Grace

 WORD PUBLISHING
Dallas London Vancouver Melbourne

WORD PUBLISHING
1996

Unless otherwise indicated, Scripture quotations used in this
book are from the Holy Bible, New Century Version, copyright © 1987, 1988,
1991 by Word Publishing, Dallas, Texas 75039. Used by permission.
Other Scripture references are from the following sources: The Holy Bible,
New International Version (NIV). Copyright © 1973, 1978, 1984 International
Bible Society. Used by permission of Zondervan Bible Publishers.
The King James Version of the Bible (KJV). *The Living Bible* (TLB),
copyright 1971 by Tyndale House Publishers, Wheaton, Ill. Used by permission.
The Message (MSG), copyright © 1993. Used by permission of
NavPress Publishing Group. The New King James Version (NKJV),
copyright © 1979, 1980, 1982, 1992, Thomas Nelson, Inc., Publisher.
J. B. Phillips: The New Testament in Modern English, Revised Edition (PHILLIPS).
Copyright © J. B. Phillips 1958, 1960, 1972. Used by permission of Macmillan
Publishing Co., Inc. The Revised Standard Version of the Bible (RSV).
Copyright © 1946, 1952, 1971, 1973 by the Division of Christian Education of the
National Council of the Churches of Christ in the USA.
Used by permission. *The Jerusalem Bible* (TJB). Copyright © 1968 by Darton,
Longman, & Todd, Ltd., and Doubleday & Co., Inc. The New
English Bible (NEB). Copyright © 1961, 1970 by the delegates of the Oxford
University Press and the Syndics of the Cambridge University Press.
Reprinted by permission.

Book design by Mark McGarry
Set in Goudy & Goudy Sans

LIBRARY OF CONGRESS CATALOGING-IN-PUBLICATION DATA
In the grip of grace / Max Lucado
p. cm.
Includes bibliographical references (p.).
ISBN 0-8499-1143-5
1. Christian life. 2. Grace (Theology) I. Title
BV4501.2.L821 1996 96-9078
248.4 — DC20
CIP

Printed in the United States of America
0 1 2 3 4 9 BVG 22 21 20

Dedicated to my editor,
Liz Heaney,
*in celebration of ten years
of words and wonder.*

Contents

Acknowledgments

Let me say a word of thanks to:

Karen Hill: My assistant and friend, what a gift you are.

Steve and Cheryl Green and the UpWords staff: Thanks for being so faithful.

Charles Prince: Our resident statesman and scholar. We treasure your input.

Charles Swindoll: Your words posted at the intersection kept me on the higher trail.

The elders, staff, and members of the Oak Hills Church of Christ: There is no church I'd rather serve.

Steve Halliday: Thanks for another excellent discussion guide.

Nancy Norris: A special salute to you for the *many* Lucado pages you've endured and improved through the years. I'm grateful.

Sue Ann Jones: May your red ink flow! Thanks for your careful editing.

My pals at Word Publishing: You've done it again! Great job.

Dr. John Stott and his insightful book *Romans: God's Good News for the World*. Your scholarship was invaluable to me as I wrote this book.

Jenna, Andrea, and Sara: I feel sorry for every dad who doesn't have you as his daughters.

And to my wife, Denalyn: Next to God's grace you're the best thing that ever happened to me.

And to you, the reader: I've prayed for you. Long before you held this book, I asked God to prepare your heart. May I ask that you pray for me? Would you offer the prayer of Colossians 4:4 on my behalf? Thank you. I'm honored that you would read these pages.

May God secure you firmly in the grip of his grace.

Introduction

My only qualification for writing a book on grace is the clothing I wear. Let me explain.

For years I owned an elegant suit complete with coat, trousers, even a hat. I considered myself quite dapper in the outfit and was confident others agreed.

The pants were cut from the cloth of my good works, sturdy fabric of deeds done and projects completed. Some studies here, some sermons there. Many people complimented my trousers, and I confess, I tended to hitch them up in public so people would notice them.

The coat was equally impressive. It was woven together from my convictions. Each day I dressed myself in deep feelings of religious fervor. My emotions were quite strong.

So strong, in fact, that I was often asked to model my cloak of zeal in public gatherings to inspire others. Of course I was happy to comply.

While there I'd also display my hat, a feathered cap of knowledge. Formed with my own hands from the fabric of personal opinion, I wore it proudly.

Surely God is impressed with my garments, I often thought. Occasionally I strutted into his presence so he could compliment the self-tailored wear. He never spoke. *His silence must mean admiration,* I convinced myself.

But then my wardrobe began to suffer. The fabric of my trousers grew thin. My best works started coming unstitched. I began leaving more undone than done, and what little I did was nothing to boast about.

No problem, I thought. *I'll work harder.*

But working harder *was* a problem. There was a hole in my coat of convictions. My resolve was threadbare. A cold wind cut into my chest. I reached up to pull my hat down firmly, and the brim ripped off in my hands.

Over a period of a few months, my wardrobe of self-righteousness completely unraveled. I went from tailored gentlemen's apparel to beggars' rags. Fearful that God might be angry at my tattered suit, I did my best to stitch it together and cover my mistakes. But the cloth was so worn. And the wind was so icy. I gave up. I went back to God. (Where else could I go?)

On a wintry Thursday afternoon, I stepped into his presence, not for applause, but for warmth. My prayer was feeble.

"I feel naked."

"You are. And you have been for a long time."

What he did next I'll never forget. "I have something to give you," he said. He gently removed the remaining threads and then picked up a robe, a regal robe, the clothing of his own goodness.

He wrapped it around my shoulders. His words to me were tender. *"My son, you are now clothed with Christ"* (see Gal. 3:27).

Though I'd sung the hymn a thousand times, I finally understood it:

> *Dressed in his righteousness alone,*
> *faultless to stand before the throne.*[1]

I have a hunch that some of you know what I'm talking about. You're wearing a handmade wardrobe yourself. You've sewn your garments, and you're sporting your religious deeds . . . and, already, you've noticed a tear in the fabric. Before you start stitching yourself together, I'd like to share some thoughts with you on the greatest discovery of my life: the grace of God.

My strategy is for us to spend some time walking the mountains of Paul's letter to the Romans. An epistle for the self-sufficient, Romans contrasts the plight of people who choose to dress in self-made garments with those who gladly accept the robes of grace. Romans is the grandest treatise on grace ever written. You'll find the air fresh and the view clear.

Martin Luther called Romans "the chief part of the New Testament and . . . truly the purest gospel."[2] God used the book to change the lives (and the wardrobes) of Luther, John Wesley, John Calvin, William Tyndale, Saint Augustine, and millions of others.

There is every reason to think he'll do the same for you.

MAX LUCADO
MEMORIAL DAY, 1996

1 The Parable of the River

Romans 1:21–32

Once there were five sons who lived in a mountain castle with their father. The eldest was an obedient son, but his four younger brothers were rebellious. Their father had warned them of the river, but they had not listened. He had begged them to stay clear of the bank lest they be swept downstream, but the river's lure was too strong.

Each day the four rebellious brothers ventured closer and closer until one son dared to reach in and feel the waters. "Hold my hand so I won't fall in," he said, and his brothers did. But when he touched the water, the current yanked him and the other three into the rapids and rolled them down the river.

Over rocks they bounced, through the

channels they roared, on the swells they rode. Their cries for help were lost in the rage of the river. Though they fought to gain their balance, they were powerless against the strength of the current. After hours of struggle, they surrendered to the pull of the river. The waters finally dumped them on the bank in a strange land, in a distant country, in a barren place.

Savage people dwelt in the land. It was not safe like their home.

Cold winds chilled the land. It was not warm like their home.

Rugged mountains marked the land. It was not inviting like their home.

Though they did not know where they were, of one fact they were sure: They were not intended for this place. For a long time the four young sons lay on the bank, stunned at their fall and not knowing where to turn. After some time they gathered their courage and reentered the waters, hoping to walk upstream. But the current was too strong. They attempted to walk along the river's edge, but the terrain was too steep. They considered climbing the mountains, but the peaks were too high. Besides, they didn't know the way.

Finally, they built a fire and sat down. "We shouldn't have disobeyed our father," they admitted. "We are a long way from home."

With the passage of time the sons learned to survive in the strange land. They found nuts for food and killed animals for skins. They determined not to forget their homeland nor abandon hopes of returning. Each day they set about the task of finding food and building shelter. Each evening they built a fire and told stories of their father and older brother. All four sons longed to see them again.

Then, one night, one brother failed to come to the fire. The others found him the next morning in the valley with the savages. He was building a hut of grass and mud. "I've grown tired of our talks," he told them. "What good does it do to remember? Besides, this land isn't so bad. I will build a great house and settle here."

"But it isn't home," they objected.

"No, but it is if you don't think of the real one."

"But what of Father?"

"What of him? He isn't here. He isn't near. Am I to spend forever awaiting his arrival? I'm making new friends; I'm learning new ways. If he comes, he comes, but I'm not holding my breath."

And so the other three left their hut-building brother and walked away. They continued to meet around the fire, speaking of home and dreaming of their return.

Some days later a second brother failed to appear at the campfire. The next morning his siblings found him on a hillside staring at the hut of his brother.

"How disgusting," he told them as they approached. "Our brother is an utter failure. An insult to our family name. Can you imagine a more despicable deed? Building a hut and forgetting our father?"

"What he's doing is wrong," agreed the youngest, "but what we did was wrong as well. We disobeyed. We touched the river. We ignored our father's warnings."

"Well, we may have made a mistake or two, but compared to the sleaze in the hut, we are saints. Father will dismiss our sin and punish him."

"Come," urged his two brothers, "return to the fire with us."

"No, I think I'll keep an eye on our brother. Someone needs to keep a record of his wrongs to show Father."

And so the two returned, leaving one brother building and the other judging.

The remaining two sons stayed near the fire, encouraging each other and speaking of home. Then one morning the youngest son awoke to find he was alone. He searched for his brother and found him near the river, stacking rocks.

"It's no use," the rock-stacking brother explained as he worked.

"Father won't come for me. I must go to him. I offended him. I insulted him. I failed him. There is only one option. I will build a path back up the river and walk into our father's presence. Rock upon rock I will stack until I have enough rocks to travel upstream to the castle. When he sees how hard I have worked and how diligent I have been, he will have no choice but to open the door and let me into his house."

The last brother did not know what to say. He returned to sit by the fire, alone. One morning he heard a familiar voice behind him. "Father has sent me to bring you home."

The youngest lifted his eyes to see the face of his oldest brother. "You have come for us!" he shouted. For a long time the two embraced.

"And your brothers?" the eldest finally asked.

"One has made a home here. Another is watching him. The third is building a path up the river."

And so Firstborn set out to find his siblings. He went first to the thatched hut in the valley.

"Go away, stranger!" screamed the brother through the window. "You are not welcome here!"

"I have come to take you home."

"You have not. You have come to take my mansion."

"This is no mansion," Firstborn countered. "This is a hut."

"It is a mansion! The finest in the lowlands. I built it with my own hands. Now, go away. You cannot have my mansion."

"Don't you remember the house of your father?"

"I have no father."

"You were born in a castle in a distant land where the air is warm and the fruit is plentiful. You disobeyed your father and ended up in this strange land. I have come to take you home."

The brother peered through the window at Firstborn as if recognizing a face he'd remembered from a dream. But the pause was brief, for suddenly the savages in the house filled the window as well. "Go away, intruder!" they demanded. "This is not your home."

"You are right," responded the firstborn son, "but neither is it his."

The eyes of the two brothers met again. Once more the hut-building brother felt a tug at his heart, but the savages had won his trust. "He just wants your mansion," they cried. "Send him away!"

And so he did.

Firstborn sought the next brother. He didn't have to walk far. On the hillside near the hut, within eyesight of the savages, sat the fault-finding son. When he saw Firstborn approaching, he shouted, "How good that you are here to behold the sin of our brother! Are you aware that he turned his back on the castle? Are you aware that he never speaks of home? I knew you would come. I have kept careful account of his deeds. Punish him! I will applaud your anger. He deserves it! Deal with the sins of our brother."

Firstborn spoke softly, "We need to deal with your sins first."

"My sins?"

"Yes, you disobeyed Father."

The son smirked and slapped at the air. "My sins are nothing. *There* is the sinner," he claimed, pointing to the hut. "Let me tell you of the savages who stay there . . ."

"I'd rather you tell me about yourself."

"Don't worry about me. Let me show you who needs help," he said, running toward the hut. "Come, we'll peek in the windows. He never sees me. Let's go together." The son was at the hut before he noticed that Firstborn hadn't followed him.

Next, the eldest son walked to the river. There he found the last brother, knee-deep in the water, stacking rocks.

"Father has sent me to take you home."

The brother never looked up. "I can't talk now. I must work."

"Father knows you have fallen. But he will forgive you . . ."

"He may," the brother interrupted, struggling to keep his balance against the current, "but I have to get to the castle first. I must build a pathway up the river. First I will show him that I am worthy. Then I will ask for his mercy."

"He has already given his mercy. I will carry you up the river. You will never be able to build a pathway. The river is too long. The task is too great for your hands. Father sent me to carry you home. I am stronger."

For the first time the rock-stacking brother looked up. "How dare you speak with such irreverence! My father will not simply forgive. I have sinned. I have sinned greatly! He told us to avoid the river, and we disobeyed. I am a great sinner. I need much work."

"No, my brother, you don't need much work. You need much grace. The distance between you and our father's house is too great. You haven't enough strength nor the stones to build the road. That is why our father sent me. He wants me to carry you home."

"Are you saying I can't do it? Are you saying I'm not strong enough? Look at my work. Look at my rocks. Already I can walk five steps!"

"But you have five million to go!"

The younger brother looked at Firstborn with anger. "I know who you are. You are the voice of evil. You are trying to seduce me from my holy work. Get behind me, you serpent!" He hurled at Firstborn the rock he was about to place in the river.

"Heretic!" screamed the path-builder. "Leave this land. You can't stop me! I will build this walkway and stand before my father, and he will have to forgive me. I will win his favor. I will earn his mercy."

Firstborn shook his head. "Favor won is no favor. Mercy earned is no mercy. I implore you, let me carry you up the river."

The response was another rock. So Firstborn turned and left.

The youngest brother was waiting near the fire when Firstborn returned.

"The others didn't come?"

"No. One chose to indulge, the other to judge, and the third to work. None of them chose our father."

"So they will remain here?"

The eldest brother nodded slowly. "For now."

"And we will return to Father?" asked the brother.

"Yes."

"Will he forgive me?"

"Would he have sent me if he wouldn't?"

And so the younger brother climbed on the back of the Firstborn and began the journey home.

*   *   *

All four brothers heard the same invitation. Each had an opportunity to be carried home by the elder brother. The first said no, choosing a grass hut over his father's house. The second said no, preferring to analyze the mistakes of his brother rather than admit his own. The third said no, thinking it wiser to make a good impression than an honest confession. And the fourth said yes, choosing gratitude over guilt.

"I'll indulge myself," resolves one son.

"I'll compare myself," opts another.

"I'll save myself," determines the third.

"I'll entrust myself to you," decides the fourth.

May I ask a vital question? As you read of the brothers, which describes your relationship to God? Have you, like the fourth son, recognized your helplessness to make the journey home alone? Do you take the extended hand of your Father? Are you caught in the grip of his grace?

Or are you like one of the other three sons?

MAPPING THE PARABLE

	The Hut-Building Hedonist Romans 1:18–32	The Fault-Finding Judgmentalist Romans 2:1–11
Strategy	indulge myself	compare myself
Goal	satisfy my passions	monitor my neighbor
Description	fun-lover	finger-pointer
Personality	laid back	stuck-up
Self-analysis	I may be bad, but so what?	I may be bad, but I'm better than . . .
Theology	disregard God	distract God
Bumper sticker	"Life is short. Play hard."	"God's watching you and so am I."
Complaint	I can't play enough.	I can't see enough.
Favorite animal	tomcat	watchdog
Spends time looking	over the menu at the options	over the fence at the neighbor
View of grace	Who, me?	Yes, you!
View of sin	No one is guilty.	He is guilty.
Work ethic	What I do is my business.	What you do is my business.
Favorite phrase	Live it up!	Straighten up!
Boundaries	If it feels good, do it.	If he feels good, note it.
Condition	bored	bitter
Paul's pronouncements	You have no excuse for the things you do.	You have no authority for the judgments you make.
Key verse	"God left them and let them go their sinful way." (1:24)	"If you think you can judge others, you are wrong. When you judge them, you are really yourself guilty because you do the same things they do." (2:1)

MAPPING THE PARABLE

The Rock-Stacking Legalist Romans 2:17–3:20	The Grace-Driven Christian Romans 3:21–25
save myself	entrust myself to Christ
measure my merits	know my father
burden-bearer	God-lover
stressed-out	peaceful
I may be bad, but if I work harder . . .	I may be bad, but I'm forgiven.
reimburse God	seek God
"I owe, I owe, it's off to work I go."	"I'm not perfect, but I'm forgiven."
I can't work enough.	I can't thank Him enough.
beaver	eagle
over the list of requirements	over the abundance of God's blessings
Not me!	Yes, me.
I'm always guilty.	I was guilty.
What God demands is my business.	What God does is my business.
Get to work!	Thank you!
If it feels good, stop it.	If it feels good, examine it.
weary	grateful
You have no solution for the problem you have.	You have no reason to fear.
". . . people cannot do any work that will make them right with God." (4:5)	". . . those who are right with God will live by trusting him." (1:17)

A hedonist. A judgmentalist. A legalist. All occupied with self to the exclusion of their father. Paul addresses these three in the first three chapters of Romans. Let's look at each one.

The Hut-Building Hedonist
Romans 1:21–32

Can you relate to the hut-builder? He traded his passion for the castle for a love of the lowland. Rather than long for home, he settled for a hut. The aim of his life is pleasure. Such is the definition of hedonism, and such is the practice of this son.

The hedonist navigates his life as if there is no father in his past, present, or future. There may have been, somewhere in the somewhat distant past, a once-upon-a-time father, but as far as the here and now? The son will live without him. There may be, in the far-away future, a father who comes and claims him, but as for today? The son will forge out his life on his own. Rather than seize the future, he's content to seize the day.

Paul had such a person in mind when he said, "They traded the glory of God who lives forever for the worship of idols made to look like earthly people, birds, animals, and snakes. . . . They worshiped and served what had been created instead of the God who created these things" (Rom. 1:23, 25). Hedonists make poor swaps; they trade mansions for huts and their brother for a stranger. They exchange their father's house for a hillside ghetto and send his son away.

The Fault-Finding Judgmentalist
Romans 2:1–11

The approach of the second brother was simple: "Why deal with my mistakes when I can focus on the mistakes of others?"

He is a judgmentalist. *I may be bad, but as long as I can find some-one worse, I am safe.* He fuels his goodness with the failures of others. He is the self-appointed teacher's pet in elementary school. He tattles on the sloppy work of others, oblivious to the F on his own paper. He's the neighborhood watchdog, passing out citations for people to clean up their act, never noticing the garbage on his own front lawn.

"Come on God, let me show you the evil deeds of my neighbor," the moralist invites. But God won't follow him into the valley. "If you think you can judge others, you are wrong. When you judge them, you are really judging yourself guilty, because you do the same things they do" (Rom. 2:1). It's a shallow ploy, and God won't fall for it.

The Rock-Stacking Legalist
Romans 2:17–3:20

And then there is the brother in the river. Ahhh, now here is a son we respect. Hard-working. Industrious. Zealous. Intense. Here is a fellow who sees his sin and sets out to resolve it by himself. Surely he is worthy of our applause. Surely he is worthy of our emulation. And, most surely, he is worthy of the father's mercy. Won't the father throw open the castle doors when he sees how hard the son has worked to get home?

With no help from the father, the legalist is tackling the odds and fording the river of failure. Surely, the father will be happy to see him. That is, if the father ever does.

You see, the problem is not the affection of the father but the strength of the river. What sucked the son away from his father's house was no gentle stream but rather a roaring torrent. Is the son strong enough to build an upriver path to the father's house?

Doubtful. We certainly can't. "There is no one who always does

what is right, not even one" (Rom. 3:10). Oh, but we try. We don't
stack rocks in a river, but we do good deeds on earth.

We think: *If I do this God will accept me.*

If I teach this class . . . and we pick up a rock.

If I go to church . . . and we put the rock in the stream.

If I give this money . . . another rock.

If I endure a Lucado book . . . ten big rocks.

*If I read my Bible, have the right opinion on the right doctrine, if I join
this movement* . . . rock upon rock upon rock.

The problem? You may take five steps, but you have five million
to go. The river is too long. What separates us from God is not a
shallow stream but a tumbling, cascading, overwhelming river of
sin. We stack and stack and stack only to find we can barely keep
our footing, much less make progress.

The impact on the rock-stackers is remarkably predictable:
either despair or arrogance. They either give up or become stuck-
up. They think they'll never make it, or they think they are the
only ones who'll ever make it. Strange, how two people can look at
the same stacked rocks and one hang his head and the other puff
out his chest.

Call the condition a *religious* godlessness. It's the theme behind
Paul's brazen pronouncement: "We're sinners, every one of us, in
the same sinking boat with everyone else" (3:19 MSG).

Godless or Godly?

Quite a trio, don't you think?

The first on a barstool.

The second in the judge's chair.

The third on the church pew.

Though they may appear different, they are very much alike. All
are separated from the Father. And none is asking for help. The

THE PARABLE OF THE RIVER 13

first indulges his passions, the second monitors his neighbor, and the third measures his merits. Self-satisfaction. Self-justification. Self-salvation. The operative word is *self*. Self-sufficient. "They never give God the time of day" (3:18 MSG).

Paul's word for this is *godlessness* (Rom. 1:18 NIV). *Godlessness.* The word defines itself. A life minus God. Worse than a disdain for God, this is a disregard for God. A disdain at least acknowledges his presence. Godlessness doesn't. Whereas disdain will lead people to act with irreverence, disregard causes them to act as if God were irrelevant, as if he is not a factor in the journey.

How does God respond to godless living? Not flippantly. "The wrath of God is being revealed from heaven against all godlessness and wickedness" (Rom. 1:18 NIV). Paul's main point is not a light one. God is justly angered over the actions of his children.

I might as well prepare you: The first chapters of Romans are not exactly upbeat. Paul gives us the bad news before he gives the good news. He will eventually tell us that we are all equal candidates for grace but not before he proves that we are all desperately sinful. We have to see the mess we are in before we can appreciate the God we have. Before presenting the grace of God, we must understand the wrath of God.

And since that is where Paul begins, that is where we will begin.

PART ONE

WHAT A MESS!

The loss of mystery has led to the loss of majesty.

The more we know, the less we believe.

No wonder there is no wonder.

We think we've figured it all out.

Strange, don't you think?

Knowledge of the workings shouldn't negate wonder.

Knowledge should stir wonder.

Who has more reason to worship than the

astronomer who has seen the stars?

Than the surgeon who has held a heart?

Than the oceanographer who has pondered the depths?

God's Gracious Anger

God's anger is shown from heaven against all the evil and wrong things people do. By their own evil lives they hide the truth. God shows his anger because some knowledge of him has been made clear to them. Yes, God has shown himself to them. ROMANS 1:18–19

"And you discovered that your boyfriend had been sleeping with your mother?" The audience snickered. The teenage girl on the stage ducked her head at the burst of attention.

The mother was a middle-aged woman in a too-tight black dress, sitting with her arm entwined with the skinny one of a boy in a sleeveless T-shirt. She waved to the crowd. He grinned.

Talk-show host Christy Adams wasted no time. "Do the two of you really sleep together?"

The mother, still holding the hand of the boy, looked at him. He grinned, and she smiled. "Yes."

She went on to explain how she'd been

lonely since her divorce. Her daughter's boyfriend hung out at her house all hours of the day and night and, well, one afternoon he plopped beside her on the couch and the two started talking and one thing led to another and the next thing she knew they were . . . Her face flushed, and the boy shrugged as they let the audience complete the sentence.

The girl sat expressionless and silent.

"Aren't you worried what this might teach your daughter?" Christy inquired.

"I'm only teaching her the ways of the world."

"What about you?" Christy asked the boy. "Aren't you being unfaithful to your girlfriend?"

The boy looked honestly amazed. "I still love her," he announced. "I'm only helping her by loving her mother. We are one happy family. There's nothing wrong with that!"

The audience erupted with whistles and applause. Just as the hubbub began to subside, Christy told the lovers, "Not everyone would agree with you. I've invited a guest to react to your lifestyle." With that, the crowd got quiet, anxious to see who Christy had recruited to spice up the dialogue.

"He's the world's most famous theologian. His writings have long been followed by some and debated by others. Making his first appearance on the Christy Adams Show, please welcome controversial theologian, scholar, and author, the apostle Paul!"

Polite applause welcomed a short, balding man with glasses and a tweed jacket. He loosened his tie a bit as he settled his small frame in the stage chair. Christy skipped the welcome. "You have trouble with what these people are doing?"

Paul held his hands in his lap, looked over at the trio, and then back at Christy. "It's not how I feel that matters. It's how God feels."

Christy paused so the TV audience could hear the "ooohs" ripple through the studio.

"Then tell us, please Paul, how does God feel about this creative tryst?"

"It angers him."

"And why?"

"Evil angers God because evil destroys his children. What these people are doing is evil."

The strong words triggered a few hoots, some scattered applause, and an outburst of raised hands. Before Christy could speak, Paul continued. "As a result God has left them and let them go their sinful way. Their thinking is dark, their acts are evil, and God is disgusted."

A lanky fellow in the front shouted out his objection. "It's her body. She can do what she wants!"

"Oh, but that's where you are mistaken. Her body belongs to God and is to be used for him."

"What we're doing is harmless," objected the mother.

"Look at your daughter," Paul urged her, gesturing toward the girl whose eyes were full of tears. "Don't you see you have harmed her? You traded healthy love for lust. You traded the love of God for the love of the flesh. You traded truth for lie. And you traded the natural for the unnatural . . . ."

Christy could restrain herself no longer. "Do you know how hokey you sound? All this talk about God and right and wrong and immorality? Don't you feel out of touch with reality?"

"Out of touch? No. Out of place, yes. But out of touch, hardly. God does not sit silently while his children indulge in perversion. He lets us go our sinful way and reap the consequences. Every broken heart, every unwanted child, every war and tragedy can be traced back to our rebellion against God."

People sprang to their feet, the mother put her finger in Paul's face, and Christy turned to the camera, delighting in the pandemonium. "We've got to take a break," she shouted over the noise.

"Don't go away; we've got some more questions for our friend the apostle."

God Hates Evil

How does the above dialogue strike you? Harsh? (Paul was too narrow.) Unreal? (The scene was too bizarre.) Outlandish? (No one would accept such convictions.)

Regardless of your response, it is important to note that though the script is fictional, Paul's words are not.

God is "against all the evil and wrong things that people do" (Rom. 1:18). The One who urges us to "hate what is evil" (Rom. 12:9) hates what is evil.

In three chilling verses Paul states:

"God left them and let them go . . ." (Rom. 1:24).
"God left them and let them do . . . " (Rom. 1:26).
"God left them and allowed them to have their own worthless thinking . . ." (Rom. 1:28).

God is angry at evil.

For many, this is a revelation. Some assume God is a harried high-school principal, too busy monitoring the planets to notice us.

He's not.

Others assume he is a doting parent, blind to the evil of his children.

Wrong.

Still others insist he loves us so much he cannot be angry at our evil.

They don't understand that love is *always* angry at evil.

God Has Every Right to Be Angry

Many don't understand God's anger because they confuse the wrath of God with the wrath of man. The two have little in common. Human anger is typically self-driven and prone to explosions of temper and violent deeds. We get ticked off because we've been overlooked, neglected, or cheated. This is the anger of man. It is not, however, the anger of God.

God doesn't get angry because he doesn't get his way. He gets angry because disobedience always results in self-destruction. What kind of father sits by and watches his child hurt himself?

What kind of God would do the same? Do we think he giggles at adultery or snickers at murder? Do you think he looks the other way when we produce television talk shows based on perverse pleasures? Does he shake his head and say, "Humans will be humans"?

I don't think so. Mark it down and underline it in red. God is rightfully angry. God is a holy God. Our sins are an affront to his holiness. His eyes "are too good to look at evil; [he] cannot stand to see those who do wrong" (Hab. 1:13).

God is angry at the evil that ruins his children. "As long as God is God, he cannot behold with indifference that his creation is destroyed and his holy will trodden underfoot."[1]

We Have No Excuse

My father had a similar hostility toward alcohol. Jack Lucado hated drinking in every form because he knew its power to destroy. His mild nature bristled at the thought of drunkenness. He left no doubt in my mind that he hated drinking and wanted his kids to have nothing to do with it.

But children don't always listen to their fathers. As a fifteen-year-old, I plotted a plan to get drunk and succeeded. I drank beer until I couldn't see straight then came home and vomited until I couldn't stand up. My father came to the bathroom, smelled the beer, threw a towel in my direction, and walked away in disgust. I stumbled back to bed, knowing I was in deep trouble.

He awoke me early the next morning. (There was no way I'd have the pleasure of sleeping off the hangover.) While in the shower I tried to think of an explanation. "My friends made me do it," or "It was an accident," or "Somebody must have put whiskey in the punch." But one option I never considered was ignorance. Never once did I think about saying, "You never told me I shouldn't get drunk."

Not only would that have been a lie, it would have been slander against my father. Had he not told me? Had he not warned me? Had he not tried to teach me? I knew better than to say that I didn't know better.

I was without excuse. According to Paul, we all are. In some of the most arresting words of the Bible he says:

> God shows his anger because some knowledge of him has been made clear to them. Yes, God has shown himself to them. There are things about him that people cannot see—his eternal power and all the things that make him God. But since the beginning of the world those things have been easy to understand by what God has made. *So people have no excuse for the bad things they do.* (Rom. 1:19–20, italics mine)

We are without excuse because God has revealed himself to us through his creation.

The psalmist wrote: "The heavens tell the glory of God, and the skies announce what his hands have made. Day after day they tell their story; night after night they tell it again. They have no speech or words; they have no voice to be heard. But their message goes through all the world; their words go everywhere on earth" (Ps. 19:1–4).

Every star is an announcement. Each leaf a reminder. The glaciers are megaphones, the seasons are chapters, the clouds are banners. Nature is a song of many parts but one theme and one verse: *God is.*

Hundreds of years ago Tertullian stated:

It was not the pen of Moses that initiated the knowledge of the Creator. . . . The vast majority of mankind, though they had never heard the name of Moses, to say nothing of his books, knew the God of Moses none-the-less. . . . Nature is the teacher; the soul is the pupil. . . . One flower of the hedgerow . . . one shell from any sea you like . . . one feather of a moor fowl . . . will they speak to you of a mean Creator? . . . If I offer you a rose, you will not scorn its Creator.[2]

Creation is God's first missionary. There are those who never held a Bible or heard a scripture. There are those who die before a translator puts God's Word in their tongue. There are millions who lived in ancient times before Christ or live in distant lands far from Christians. There are the simple-minded who are incapable of understanding the gospel. What does the future hold for the person who never hears of God?

Again, Paul's answer is clear. The human heart can know God through the handiwork of nature. If that is all one ever sees, that is enough. One need only respond to what he is given. And if he is given only the testimony of creation, then he has enough.

The problem is not that God hasn't spoken but that we haven't listened. God says his anger is directed against any *thing* and any *one* who suppresses the knowledge of truth. God loves his children, and he hates what destroys them. This doesn't mean that he flies into a rage or loses his temper or is emotionally unpredictable. It means simply that he loves you and hates what you become when you turn from him.

Call it holy hostility. A righteous hatred of wrong. A divine disgust at the evil that destroys his children.

The question is not, "How dare a loving God be angry?" but rather, "How could a loving God feel anything less?"

Godless Living

Romans 1:21–32

*They traded the glory of God who lives
forever for the worship of idols made to look like
earthly people, birds, animals, and snakes. . . .
They worshiped and served what had been
created instead of the God who created
those things.* ROMANS 1:23, 25

Can a cricket comprehend communion? I've
been pondering this question since last
Sunday, when both the cricket and the question
came my way. The Lord's Supper was
being served when I bowed my head and
noticed the visitor beneath my pew. Best I
can figure, he'd sneaked in a side door,
slipped between the deacon's feet, and
worked his way to the front of the sanctuary.

The sight of a cricket stirs many emotions
within me, not one of them spiritual. Forgive
me, all you bug lovers, but I'm not attracted
to his beauty nor stunned by his strength.
Typically I would have no interest in the
insect, but the sight of a bug in an auditorium strikes me as symbolic.

We have something in common, you, me, and the cricket. Limited vision. I hope the parallel doesn't bug you (*ouch!*), but I think it's fair. None of us do too well imagining life beyond the rafters.

You see, as far as the cricket is concerned, his entire universe is an auditorium. I can envision him taking his son out of the wall at night and telling him to look up at the rafters. He wraps his clickers around the boy's back and sighs, "It's a mighty sky we live under, son." Does he know he sees only a fraction?

And then there are the aspirations of a cricket. His highest dream is to find a piece of bread. He falls asleep with visions of pie crumbs and jam drippings.

Or consider the hero of the cricket's world. Crickets lionize bugs. A fast one who can dash across a room full of feet. A gutsy one who has explored the hinterlands of the baptistry. A courageous one who has ventured to the edge of a mighty cabinet or hopped along the precipice of a window sill. Is there, in the legends of cricketdom, a story about Cricket Revere who dashed through the walls yelling, "The bugman is coming! The bugman is coming!"?

Do amazed crickets ever look at each other and proclaim, "Jimminy Human!"?

Perhaps the best question is, who does a cricket worship? Does he acknowledge that there was a hand behind the building? Or does he choose to worship the building itself? Or perhaps a place in the building? Does he assume that since he has never seen the builder there *was* no builder?

The hedonist does. Since he has never seen the hand who made the universe, he assumes there is no life beyond the here and now. He believes there is no truth beyond this room. No purpose beyond his own pleasure. No divine factor. He has no concern for the eternal. Like a cricket who refuses to acknowledge a builder, he refuses to acknowledge his creator.

The hedonist opts to live as if there is no creator at all. Again, Paul's word for this is *godlessness*. He wrote, "People did not think it was important to have a true knowledge of God" (Rom. 1:28).

What happens when a society sees the world through the eyes of a cricket? What happens when a culture settles for grass huts instead of the father's castle? Are there any consequences for a godless pursuit of pleasure? Is there a price to pay for living for today?

The hedonist says, "Who cares? I may be bad, but so what? What I do is my business." He's more concerned about satisfying his passions than in knowing the Father. His life is so desperate for pleasure that he has no time or room for God.

Is he right? Is it OK to spend our days thumbing our noses at God and living it up?

Paul says, "Absolutely not!"

According to Romans 1, we lose more than stained-glass windows when we dismiss God. We lose our standard, our purpose, and our worship. "Their thinking became useless. Their foolish minds were filled with darkness. They said they were wise, but they became fools" (Rom. 1:21–22).

1. We Lose Our Standard

When I was nine years old I complimented a friend's model airplane. He curtly replied, "I stole it." He could tell that I was stunned because he asked, "Do you think that was wrong?"

When I told him I did, he answered simply, "It may be wrong for you. It's not wrong for me. I didn't hurt anyone when I stole the plane. I knew the owner. He is rich. I'm not. He can afford one. I can't."

What do you say to that argument? If you don't believe in life beyond the rafters, you have little to say. If there is no ultimate good *behind* the world, then how do we define "good" *within* the world? If the majority opinion determines good and evil, what happens when the majority is wrong? What do you do when the majority of kids in a certain group say it's all right to steal or raid or even fire pistols from a moving vehicle?

The hedonist's world of no moral absolutes works fine on paper and sounds great in a college philosophy course, but in life? Ask the father of three children whose wife abandoned him, saying, "Divorce may be wrong for you, but it's OK for me." Or get the opinion of the teenage girl, pregnant and frightened, who was told by her boyfriend, "If you have the baby, it's your responsibility." Or the retirees ripped off of their pension by a huckster who believed anything is right if you don't get caught.

A godly view of the world, on the other hand, has something to say to my childhood thief. Faith challenges those with cricket brains to answer to a higher standard than personal opinion: "You may think it's right. Society may think it's OK. But the God who made you said, 'You shall not steal'—and he wasn't kidding."

By the way, follow the godless thinking to its logical extension, and see what you get. What happens when a society denies the importance of right and wrong? Read the answer on a prison wall in Poland: "I freed Germany from the stupid and degrading fallacies of conscience and morality." [1]

Who made the boast? Adolf Hitler. Where are the words posted? In a Nazi death camp. Visitors read the claim and then see its results: a room stuffed with thousands of pounds of women's hair, rooms filled with pictures of castrated children and gas ovens that served as Hitler's final solution. Paul described it best: "Their foolish minds were filled with darkness" (Rom. 1:21).

Come on, Max, you're going too far. Isn't it a stretch to state that what began as a stolen model plane will conclude in a holocaust?

Most of the time it won't. But it could, and what is there to stop it? What dike does the God-denying thinker have to stop the flood? What anchor will the secularist use to keep society from being sucked out to sea? If a society deletes God from the human equation, what sandbags will it stack against the swelling tide of barbarism and hedonism?

As Dostoevsky stated, "If God is dead, then everything is justifiable."

2. We Lose Our Purpose

The following conversation occurred between a canary in a cage and a lark on the window sill. The lark looked in at the canary and asked, "What is your purpose?"

"My purpose is to eat seed."

"What for?"

"So I can be strong."

"What for?"

"So I can sing," answered the canary.

"What for?" continued the lark.

"Because when I sing I get more seed."

"So you eat in order to be strong so you can sing so you can get seed so you can eat?"

"Yes."

"There is more to you than that," the lark offered. "If you'll follow me I'll help you find it, but you must leave your cage."

It's tough to find meaning in a caged world. But that doesn't keep us from trying. Mine deep enough in every heart and you'll find it: a longing for meaning, a quest for purpose. As surely as a child breathes, he will someday wonder, "What is the purpose of my life?"

Some search for meaning in a career. "My purpose is to be a dentist." Fine vocation but hardly a justification for existence. They opt to be a human "doing" rather than a human "being." Who they are is what they do; consequently they do a lot. They work many hours because if they don't work, they don't have an identity.

For others, who they are is what they have. They find meaning in a new car or a new house or new clothes. These people are great for the economy and rough on the budget because they are always seeking meaning in something they own.

Still others seek meaning in who they sire. They live vicariously through their kids. Woe be unto these kids. It's hard enough being a youngster without also being someone's reason for living.

Some try sports, entertainment, cults, sex, you name it.

All mirages in the desert of purpose. "Claiming themselves to be wise without God, they became utter fools instead" (Rom. 1:22 TLB).

Shouldn't we face the truth? If we don't acknowledge God, we are flotsam in the universe. At best we are developed animals. At worst we are rearranged space dust. In the final analysis secularists have only one answer to the question, "What is the meaning of life?" Their answer? "We don't know."

Or as paleontologist Stephen J. Gould concluded:

> We are because one odd group of fishes had a peculiar fin anatomy that could transform into legs for terrestrial creatures; because the earth never froze entirely during an ice age; because a small and tenuous species, arising in Africa a quarter of million years ago, had managed, so far, to survive by hook and by crook. We may yearn for a 'higher' answer—but none exists.[2]

Sacrificed upon the altar of godlessness is the purpose of man.

Contrast that to God's vision for life: "We are God's handiwork, created in Christ Jesus to devote ourselves to the good deeds for which God has designed us" (Eph. 2:10 NEB).

With God in your world, you aren't an accident or an incident; you are a gift to the world, a divine work of art, signed by God.

One of the finest gifts I ever received is a football signed by thirty former professional quarterbacks. There is nothing unique about this ball. For all I know it was bought at a discount sports store. What makes it unique is the signatures.

The same is true with us. In the scheme of nature *Homo sapiens* are not unique. We aren't the only creatures with flesh and hair and blood and hearts. What makes us special is not our body but the signature of God on our lives. We are his works of art. We are created in his image to do good deeds. We are significant, not because of what we do, but because of whose we are.

3. We Lose Our Worship

You've heard the story of the man searching for his keys under the street light? His friend sees him and stops to help. After some minutes he asks, "Exactly where did you drop your keys?"

"In my house," the man answers.

"In your house? Then why are we looking out here?"

"Because the light is better out here."

You'll never find what you need if you don't look in the right place. If you're looking for keys, go where you lost them. If you're looking for truth and purpose, go outside the rafters. And if you're looking for the sacred, once again, you won't find it by thinking like a cricket.

"They traded the glory of God who holds the whole world in his hands for any cheap figurines you can buy at any roadside stand" (Rom. 1:21 MSG).

Let's return to the crickets for a moment. Assume that these crickets are quite advanced and often engage in the philosophical question, "Is there life beyond the rafters?"

Some crickets believe there is. There must be a creator of this place. How else would the lights come on? How else could air blow through the vents? How else could music fill the room? Out of

their amazement for what they see, they worship what they can't
see.

But other crickets disagree. Upon study they find the lights
come on because of electricity. The air blows because of air condi-
tioners, and music is the result of stereos and speakers. "There is no
life beyond this room," they declare. "We have figured out how
everything works."

Would we let the crickets get by with that? Of course not! "Just
because you understand the system," we'd tell them, "that doesn't
deny the presence of someone outside the system. After all, who
built it? Who installed the switch? Who diagrammed the compres-
sor and engineered the generator?

But don't we make the same mistake? We understand how storms
are created. We map solar systems and transplant hearts. We measure the depths of the oceans and send signals to distant planets. We
crickets have studied the system and are learning how it works.

And, for some, the loss of mystery has led to the loss of majesty.
The more we know, the less we believe. Strange, don't you think?
Knowledge of the workings shouldn't negate wonder. Knowledge
should stir wonder. Who has more reason to worship than the
astronomer who has seen the stars? Than the surgeon who has held
a heart? Than the oceanographer who has pondered the depths?
The more we know, the more we should be amazed.

Ironically, the more we know, the less we worship. We are more
impressed with our discovery of the light switch than with the one
who invented electricity. Call it cricket-brained logic. Rather than
worship the Creator, we worship the creation (see Rom. 1:25).

No wonder there is no wonder. We've figured it all out.

One of the most popular attractions at Disney World is the
Jungle Cruise. People will spend forty-five minutes waiting in the
Florida heat for the chance to board the boat and wind through
snake-infested forests. They come for the thrills. You never know

when a native will jump out of the trees or a crocodile will peek out of the water. The waterfalls drench you, the rainbow inspires you, and the baby elephants playing in the water amuse you.

It's quite a trip—the first few times. But after four or five runs down the river, it begins to lose its zest. I should know. During the three years I lived in Miami, Florida, I made nearly twenty trips to Orlando. I was single and owned a van and was a sucker for any-body who wanted to spend a day at the Magic Kingdom. By the eighth or ninth trip I could tell you the names of the guides and the jokes they told.

A couple of times I actually dozed off on the journey. The trail had lost its secrets. Ever wonder why people sleep in on Sunday mornings (whether in the bed or in the sanctuary)? Now you know. They've seen it all. Why get excited? They know it all. There is nothing sacred. The holy becomes humdrum. Rather than dashing into life like kids to the park, we doze through our days like com-muters on a train.

Can you see why people become "full of sexual sin, using our bodies wrongly with each other"? (Rom. 1:24). You've got to get excitement somewhere.

According to Romans 1, godlessness is a bad swap. In living for today, the hut-building hedonist destroys his hope of living in a castle tomorrow.

What was true in Paul's day is still true in ours, and we would do well to heed his warning. Otherwise, what is to keep us from destroying ourselves? If there is no standard in this life, no purpose to this life, and nothing sacred about this life, what is to keep us from doing whatever we want?"

"Nothing," said one cricket to the other.

How does God feel about such a view of life? Let me give you a hint. How would you feel if you saw your children settling for crumbs when you'd prepared for them a feast?

4 Godless Judging

Romans 2:1–11

If you think you can judge others, you are wrong. When you judge them, you are really judging yourself guilty, because you do the same things they do. God judges those who do wrong things, and we know that his judging is right. ROMANS 2:1

You know what disturbs me most about Jeffrey Dahmer?

What disturbs me most are not his acts, though they are disgusting. Dahmer was convicted of seventeen murders. Eleven corpses were found in his apartment. He cut off arms. He ate body parts. My thesaurus has 204 synonyms for *vile*, but each falls short of describing a man who kept skulls in his refrigerator and hoarded a human heart. He redefined the boundary for brutality. The Milwaukee monster dangled from the lowest rung of human conduct and then dropped. But that's not what troubles me most.

Can I tell you what troubles me most about Jeffrey Dahmer? Not his trial, as disturbing as it was, with all those pictures of him sitting serenely in court, face frozen, motionless. No sign of remorse, no hint of regret. Remember his steely eyes and impassive face? But I don't speak of him because of his trial. There is another reason. Can I tell you what really troubles me about Jeffrey Dahmer?

Not his punishment, though life without parole is hardly an exchange for his actions. How many years would satisfy justice? A lifetime in jail for every life he took? But that's another matter, and that's not what troubles me most about Jeffrey Dahmer. May I tell you what does?

His conversion.

Months before an inmate murdered him, Jeffrey Dahmer became a Christian. Said he repented. Was sorry for what he did. Profoundly sorry. Said he put his faith in Christ. Was baptized. Started life over. Began reading Christian books and attending chapel.

Sins washed. Soul cleansed. Past forgiven.

That troubles me. It shouldn't, but it does. Grace for a cannibal?

Maybe you have the same reservations. If not about Dahmer perhaps about someone else. Ever wrestled with the deathbed conversion of a rapist or the eleventh-hour conversion of a child molester? We've sentenced them, maybe not in court, but in our hearts. We've put them behind bars and locked the door. They are forever imprisoned by our disgust. And then, the impossible happens. They repent.

Our response? (Dare we say it?) We cross our arms and furrow our brows and say, "God won't let you off that easy. Not after what you did. God is kind, but he's no wimp. Grace is for average sinners like me, not deviants like you."

And for proof we might turn to Romans 1. "*God's anger is being shown against . . .*" And then Paul lists it all: sexual sin, evil, self-ishness, hatred, jealousy, murder (see 1:26–30). We want to shout,

"Go get 'em, Paul! It's about time someone spoke out against sin! It's high time someone pulled back the blanket on adultery and turned the light on dishonesty. Nail those perverts. String up those porn peddlers. We'll stand by you, Paul! We decent, law-abiding folk are with you!"

Paul's response?

"If you think that leaves you on the high ground where you can point your finger at others, think again. Every time you criticize someone, you condemn yourself. It takes one to know one" (Rom. 2:1 MSG).

Whoops!

Having addressed the hut-building tomcat, he turns his torch on the hillside watchdog.

We Don't Hold the Gavel

In Romans 1 Paul confronts the hedonists. In chapter 2 he deals with another group, the judgmental moralists: those who, "pass judgment on someone else" (2:1 NIV). Somewhere between the escort service and the church service there is the person who "points [his] finger at others" (2:1 MSG).

"Therefore you have no excuse, O man, whoever you are, when you judge another; for in passing judgment upon him you condemn yourself, because you, the judge, are doing the very same things" (2:1 RSV).

Who is this person? It could be anyone ("O man, whoever you are") who filters God's grace through his own opinion. Anyone who dilutes God's mercy with his own prejudice. He is the prodigal son's elder brother who wouldn't attend the party (see Luke 15:11–32). He is the ten-hour worker, upset because the one-hour worker got the same wage (see Matt. 20:1–16). He is the fault-finding brother obsessed by his brother's sins and oblivious to his own.

If you "think you can judge others" (Rom. 2:1), Paul has a stern reminder for you. It's not your job to hold the gavel. "God judges those who do wrong things, and we know that his judging is right" (v. 2).

The key word here is *judges*. It's one thing to have an opinion. It's quite another to pass a verdict. It's one thing to have a conviction; it's another to convict the person. It's one thing to be repulsed at the acts of a Jeffrey Dahmer (and I am.) It's another entirely to claim that I am superior (I'm not) or that he is beyond the grace of God (no one is.)

As John Stott writes: "This [verse] is not a call either to suspend our critical faculties or to renounce all criticism and rebuke of others as illegitimate: it is rather a prohibition of standing in judgment on other people and condemning them (which as human beings we have no right to do), especially when we fail to condemn ourselves."[1]

It's our job to hate the sin. But it's God's job to deal with the sinner. God has called us to despise evil, but he's never called us to despise the evildoer.

But, oh, how we would like to. Is there any act more delightful than judging others? There is something smug and self-satisfying about donning the robe, stepping behind the bench, and slamming down the gavel. "Guilty!"

Besides, judging others is the quick and easy way to feel good about ourselves. A convenience-store ego-boost. Standing next to all the Mussolinis and Hitlers and Dahmers of the world, we boast, "Look, God, compared to them, I'm not too bad."

But that's the problem. God doesn't compare us to them. They aren't the standard. God is. And compared to him, Paul will argue, "There is no one who does anything good" (Rom. 3:12). In fact, that is one of two reasons why God is the One who judges.

Reason #1: We Aren't Good Enough

Suppose God simplified matters and reduced the Bible to one command: "Thou must jump so high in the air that you touch the moon." No need to love your neighbor or pray or follow Jesus; just touch the moon by virtue of a jump, and you'll be saved.

We'd never make it. There may be a few who jump three or four feet, even fewer who jump five or six; but compared to the distance we have to go, no one gets very far. Though you may jump six inches higher than I do, it's scarcely reason to boast.

Now, God hasn't called us to touch the moon, but he might as well have. He said, "You must be perfect, just as your Father in heaven is perfect" (Matt. 5:48). None of us can meet God's standard. As a result, none of us deserves to don the robe and stand behind the bench and judge others. Why? We aren't good enough. Dahmer may jump six inches, and you may jump six feet, but compared to the 230,000 miles that remain, who can boast?

The thought of it is almost comical. We who jump three feet look at the fellow who jumped one inch and say, "What a lousy jump." Why do we engage in such accusations? It's a ploy. As long as I am thinking of your weaknesses, then I don't have to think about mine. As long as I am looking at your puny jump, then I don't have to be honest about my own. I'm like the man who went to see the psychiatrist with a turtle on his head and a strip of bacon dangling from each ear and said, "I'm here to talk to you about my brother."

It's the universal strategy of impunity. Even kids use it. *If I can get Dad more angry at my brother than me, I'm off scot-free.* So I accuse. I compare. Rather than admit my own faults, I find faults in others. The easiest way to justify the mistakes in my house is to find worse ones in my neighbor's house.

Such scams don't work with God. Read carefully Paul's words.

God isn't so easily diverted. He sees right through all smoke screens and holds you to what *you've* done. You didn't think, did you, that just by pointing your finger at others you would distract God from coming down on you hard? Or did you think that just because he's such a nice God he'd let you off the hook? Better think this one through from the beginning. God is kind, but he's not soft. In kindness he takes us firmly by the hand and leads us into a radical life change. (Rom. 2:2–4 MSG)

We aren't good enough to judge. Can the hungry accuse the beggar? Can the sick mock the ill? Can the blind judge the deaf? Can the sinner condemn the sinner? No. Only One can judge, and that One is neither writing nor reading this book.

Reason #2: We Don't Know Enough

Not only are we unworthy, we are unqualified. We don't know enough about the person to judge him. We don't know enough about his past. We condemn a man for stumbling this morning, but we didn't see the blows he took yesterday. We judge a woman for the limp in her walk but cannot see the tack in her shoe. We mock the fear in their eyes but have no idea how many stones they have ducked or darts they have dodged.

Are they too loud? Perhaps they fear being neglected again. Are they too timid? Perhaps they fear failing again. Too slow? Perhaps they fell the last time they hurried. You don't know. Only one who has followed yesterday's steps can be their judge.

Not only are we ignorant about yesterday, we are ignorant about tomorrow. Dare we judge a book while chapters are yet unwritten? Should we pass a verdict on a painting while the artist still holds the brush? How can you dismiss a soul until God's work is complete? "God began doing a good work in you, and I am sure he will continue it until it is finished when Jesus Christ comes again" (Phil. 1:6).

Be careful! The Peter who denies Jesus at tonight's fire may proclaim him with fire at tomorrow's Pentecost. The Samson who is blind and weak today may use his final strength to level the pillars of godlessness. A stammering shepherd in this generation may be the mighty Moses of the next. Don't call Noah a fool, you may be asking him for a lift. "Do not judge before the right time; wait until the Lord comes" (1 Cor. 4:5).

A condemned criminal was sent to his death by his country. In his final moments, he asked for mercy. Had he asked for mercy from the people, it would have been denied. Had he asked it of the government, it would have been declined. Had he asked it of his victims, they would have turned a deaf ear. But it wasn't to these he turned for grace. He turned instead to the bloodied form of the One who hung on the cross next to his and pleaded, "Jesus, remember me when you come into your kingdom." And Jesus answered by saying, "I tell you the truth, today you will be with me in paradise" (Luke 23:43).

As far as we know, Jeffrey Dahmer did the same thing. And as far as we know, Jeffrey Dahmer got the same response. And when you think about it, the request Dahmer made is no different than yours or mine. He may make it from a prison bunk and you may make it from a church pew, but from heaven's angle we're all asking for the moon.

And by heaven's grace we all receive it.

Godless Religion

Romans 2:17–3:18

*You call yourself a Jew. You trust in the law
of Moses and brag that you are close to God.
. . . You think you know everything and have
all truth. You teach others, so why don't you
teach yourself?* ROMANS 2:17, 20–21

Suppose I invite you to go sailing with me.

"I didn't know you were a sailor," you observe.

"You bet your barnacles I am," I answer.

"Tell me, where did you learn to sail?"

I flash a cocky smile and pull a faded photo out of my pocket. You look at the sailor standing on the bow of a schooner. "That's my great-grandpa. He sailed Cape Horn. Sailing is in my blood. I got saltwater in my veins."

"Your great-grandpa taught you how to sail?"

"Of course not. He died before I was born."

"Then who taught you to sail?"

I produce a leather-bound book and boast, "I read the manual."

"You read a book on sailing?"

"More than that. I took a course at the community college. I can tell you the difference between fore and aft, and I can show you the stern and the bow. I can tie a square knot. You ought to see me hoist a mast."

"You mean, 'hoist a sail'?"

"Whatever. We even went on a field trip, and I met a real captain. I shook his hand! Come on, you want to sail?"

"Honestly, Max, I don't think you are a sailor."

"You want the proof? You want the *real* proof? Take a look, matey, I've got a gen-u-ine tattoo." I roll up my sleeve revealing a mermaid sitting on an anchor. "Watch how she jumps when I flex."

You aren't impressed. "That's all the proof you have?"

"What else do I need? I've got the pedigree. I've got the book. And I've got the tattoo. All aboard!"

Chances are you'd stay on shore. Even a landlubber knows it takes more than a family tree, a night course, and ink-stained skin to be seaworthy. You wouldn't trust a fellow like me to sail your boat, and Paul wouldn't trust a fellow like me to navigate the church.

Apparently some were trying. Oh, they weren't the seafaring type, they were the religious type. Their ancestors weren't shipmates; they were pew mates. They didn't have a book on boats, but they had a book called the Torah. And most of all, they'd been tattooed; they'd been circumcised. And they were proud; proud of their lineage, their law, and their initiation.

My hunch is they were also proud of Paul's letter. Imagine the congregation listening to this epistle. Jews on one side, Gentiles on the other. Can't you see the Jews beaming? Paul speaks out against the godless deviants, and they nod. Paul warns of the divine wrath directed at hedonist hut-builders, and they smile. As Paul, their fellow Jew, lambastes the evil uncircumcised, they erupt in a chorus, "Amen! Paul. Preach it!"

But then Paul surprises them.

He pokes his finger at their puffy chests and asks,

What about you? You call yourself a Jew. You trust in the law of Moses and brag that you are close to God. You know what he wants you to do and what is important, because you have learned the law. You think you are a guide for the blind and a light for those who are in darkness. You think you can show foolish people what is right and teach those who know nothing. You have the law; so you think you know everything and have all truth. (Rom. 2:17–20)

Don't Put Pride in Your Pedigree

Those aren't fireworks you are hearing; they are bombshells. Seven bombshells to be exact. Seven heat-seeking verbs launched into the midst of legalism. Listen as they explode.

"You *call* yourself a Jew."

"You *trust* in the law of Moses and *brag* that you are close to God."

"You *know* what he wants you to do and what is important because you have learned the law."

"You *think* you are a guide for the blind and a light for those who are in darkness."

"You *think* you can show foolish people what is right and teach those who know nothing."

". . . you *think* you know everything" (see 2:17–20).

Boom. Boom. Boom. Just when the deacons thought they were going to get praised, they got blasted. Paul tells them, "Some Jews you are. You trust in the law rather than the lawgiver and brag that you have a monopoly on God. You're convinced you are a part of a prized few who 'know' (beyond a shadow of a doubt) what God wants you to do. If that's not bad enough, you 'think' you are God's gift to the confused and the foolish. In fact, you 'think' you know everything."

Something tells me Paul just blew his shot at the "Clergyman of the Year" award. The apostle, however, is more concerned about making a point than about scoring points, and his point for religious rock-stackers is clear: "Don't put pride in your pedigree." Being born with a silver mezuzah in your mouth means nothing in heaven. Faith is intensely personal. There is no royal lineage or holy bloodline in God's kingdom.

The story of the lumberjack's son comes to mind. Somehow the youngster became convinced that there were ghosts in the forest. This disturbed his father, who made a living among the trees and wanted his son to do the same. To comfort his son the father gave him his scarf, saying, "The ghosts are afraid of me, my son. Wear this scarf, and the ghosts will be afraid of you. The scarf will make you a lumberjack."

And so the son did. He wore the scarf proudly, telling all who would listen that he was a lumberjack. Still, he never entered the forest, and he never cut a tree, but since he had his father's scarf, he considered himself a lumberjack.

The father would have been wiser to teach his son there were no ghosts rather than to teach him to trust in a scarf.

The Jews trusted the scarves of their fathers. They rode on the coattails of their heritage. Didn't matter that they were thieves, adulterers, and extortionists (see Rom. 2:22–23); they still considered themselves God's chosen few. Why? Because they had the scarf.

Maybe you were given a scarf. Perhaps the branches of your family tree are heavy with saints and seers. Perhaps you were born in a church basement and cut your teeth on a pew. If so, be grateful, but don't be lazy. Better to trust the truth than the scarf.

Or maybe you have no pedigree. Your ancestry is more like a lineup at the county jail than a roster of Sunday school teachers. If so, don't worry. Just as religious heritage brings no bonus points, a secular heritage brings no deficits. Family trees can't save you or condemn you; the ultimate decision is yours.

Don't Trust a Symbol

Having dealt with the problem of pedigree, Paul now addresses the problem of the tattoo. He turns his attention to the most sacred badge of the Jew: circumcision. Circumcision symbolized the nearness God desires with his people. God puts a knife to our self-sufficiency. He wants to be a part of our identity, our intimacy, and even our potency. Circumcision proclaimed that there is no part of our life too private or too personal for God.

Yet, rather than see circumcision as a sign of submission, the Jews had come to see it as a sign of superiority. With time they began to trust the symbol more than the Father. Paul shatters this illusion by proclaiming, "True circumcision is not only on the outside of the body. A person is a Jew only if he is a Jew inside; true circumcision is done in the heart by the Spirit, not by the written law. Such a person gets praise from God rather than from people" (Rom. 2:28–29).

Later Paul asks, "Did God accept Abraham before or after he was circumcised?" (Rom. 4:10). Important question. If God only accepted Abraham after the circumcision, then Abraham was accepted according to his merit and not according to his faith.

What is Paul's answer? Abraham was accepted "before his circumcision" (v. 10). Abraham was accepted by God in Genesis 15 and circumcised in Genesis 17. Fourteen years separate the two events!

If Abraham was already accepted by God, then why was he circumcised? Paul answers the question in the next verse: "Abraham was circumcised to show that he was right with God through faith before he was circumcised" (v. 11).

Paul point is crucial: Circumcision was symbolic. Its purpose was to show what God had already done.

I see a great example of this as I type these words. On my left hand is a symbol—a gold ring. Though not elaborate, it's priceless. It cost a pretty, young fourth-grade schoolteacher two hundred dollars. She gave it to me the day we married. The ring is a symbol of our love, a statement of our love, a declaration of our love, but it is not the source of our love.

When we have spats or trouble, I don't take off the ring and set it on a pedestal and pray to it. I don't rub it and seek wisdom. Were I to lose the ring, I'd be disappointed, but our marriage would continue. It is a symbol, nothing more.

Suppose I tried to make the ring more than it is. Suppose I became a jerk of a husband, cruel and unfaithful. Imagine that I failed to provide for Denalyn's needs or care for our children. What if one day she reached the breaking point and said, "You are not a husband to me. There is no love in your heart or devotion in your life. I want you to leave."

How do you think she'd respond if I countered, "How dare you say that? I'm wearing the ring you gave me. I've never removed it one minute! Sure I beat you and cheated on you, but I wore the ring. Isn't that enough?"

How many of you think such a defense would move her to apologize and weep, "Oh, Max, how forgetful of me. You have been so sacrificial wearing that ring all these years. Sure you have beaten me, abandoned me, neglected me, but I'll dismiss all that because you have worn the ring"?

Hogwash. She'd never say that. Why? Because apart from love, the ring means nothing. The symbol represents love, but it cannot replace love. Paul is accusing the Jews of trusting the symbol of circumcision while neglecting their souls. Could he accuse us of the same error?

Substitute a contemporary symbol such as baptism or communion or church membership.

"God, I know I never think about you. I know I hate people and cheat my friends. I abuse my body and lie to my spouse. But you don't mind, do you? I mean after all, I was baptized at that Christian camp when I was ten years old."

Or, "Every Easter I take communion."

Or, "My father and mother were fifth generation Presbyterians, you know."

Do you think God would say, "You're right. You never think of me or respect me. You hate your neighbor and abuse your kids, but since you were baptized, I will overlook your rebellion and evil ways"?

Hogwash. A symbol has no power apart from the ones who share it.

In my closet is a varsity football jacket. I earned it by playing two years of high-school football. It, too, is a symbol. It's symbolic of sweat and work and long hours on the practice field. The jacket and a sore knee are reminders of something I could do twenty years ago. Do you think if I put the jacket on now I'd instantly be twenty pounds lighter and a whole lot faster? Do you think if I wore that jacket into the office of a coach he'd extend his hand and say, "We've been waiting for a player like you. Go out there and suit up!"?

Hogwash. That jacket is merely a memoir of something I once did. It says nothing about what I could do today. It alone doesn't transform me, empower me, or enable me.

Neither does your heritage, even if you're a descendant of John Wesley.

Neither does your communion service, even if you double up on the wafers.

Neither does your baptism, even if you got dunked in the Jordan River.

Please understand. Symbols are important. Some of them, like communion and baptism, illustrate the cross of Christ. They symbolize salvation, demonstrate salvation, even articulate salvation. But they do not impart salvation.

Putting your trust in a symbol is like claiming to be a sailor because you have a tattoo or claiming to be a good husband because you have a ring or claiming to be a football player because you have a letter jacket.

Do we honestly think God would save his children based upon a symbol?

What kind of God would look at a religious hypocrite and say, "You've never loved me, sought me or obeyed me, but because your name was on the roll of a church in the right denomination I will save you"?

On the other hand, what kind of God would look at the sincere seeker and say, "You dedicated your life to loving me and loving my children. You surrendered your heart and confessed your sins. I want to save you so badly. I'm so sorry, your church took communion one time a month too many. Because of a technicality, you are forever lost in hell"?

Hogwash. Our God is abundant in love and steadfast in mercy. He saves us, not because we trust in a symbol, but because we trust in a Savior.

Please note Paul hasn't changed subjects; he's just changed audiences. His topic is still the tragedy of a godless life. "The wrath of God is being revealed from heaven against all the godlessness" (Rom. 1:18 NIV).

From God's perspective there is no difference between the ungodly party-goer, the ungodly finger-pointer, and the ungodly pew-sitter. The *Penthouse* gang, the courthouse clan, and the church choir need the same message: Without God all are lost.

Or as Paul summarizes:

All of us, whether insiders or outsiders, start out in identical conditions, which is to say we all start out as sinners. Scripture leaves no doubt about it: "There's nobody living right, not even one, nobody who knows the score, nobody alert for God." (Rom. 3:10 MSG)

Just as lineage, laws, and tattoos don't make me a sailor, heritage, rituals, and ceremonies don't make me a Christian. "God justifies the believer, not because of the worthiness of his belief, but because of [Christ's] worthiness."[1]

Don't Try to Do What Only God Can Do

Let's go back to my sailing invitation. I know I said you probably wouldn't go, but let's pretend that you aren't as smart as you look, and you accept and board the boat.

You begin to worry when you notice that I lift the sail only a few inches on the mast. You think it even stranger that I position myself behind the partially raised sail and begin to blow.

"Why don't you raise the sail?" you ask.

"Because I can't blow on the whole thing," I pant.

"Let the wind blow it," you urge.

"Oh, I can't do that. I'm sailing this boat by myself."

Those are the words of a legalist, huffing and puffing to push his vessel to heaven. (Ever wonder why so many religious folk seem out of breath?)

With time we drift out to sea, and a powerful storm hits. Rain splatters on the deck, and the little vessel bounces on the waves. "I'm going to set the anchor!" I yell. You're relieved that I at least know where the anchor is, but then you are stunned at where I put it.

First, I take the anchor and set it up near the bow. "That should steady the boat!" I shout. But, of course, it doesn't. Next I carry the anchor to the stern. "Now we are secure!" But the bouncing continues. I hang the anchor on the mast, but it doesn't help. Finally, in fear and frustration, you take the anchor and throw it out to the deep and scream, "Don't you know you have to anchor to something other than yourself!"

A legalist doesn't know that. He anchors only to himself. His security comes from what he does; his lineage, his law, and his tattoo. When the storm blows the legalist casts his anchor on his own works. He will save himself. After all, isn't he in the right group? Doesn't he have the right law? And hasn't he passed through the right initiation? (Ever wonder why so many religious people have such stormy lives?)

Here is the point: Salvation is God's business.

Remember the parable of the river? The first brother, the hedonist, built a hut and called it a mansion. The second brother, the judgmentalist, watched him and called him a deviant. A legalist, the third brother stacked rocks and relied upon his own strength. He represents the godless religionist who stacks his good deeds against the current, thinking they will make a path upstream. In the end all three reject the invitation of the firstborn son, and all are equally distant from the father.

The message of the parable and Paul's message in Romans are

the same: God is the One who saves his children. There is only one name under heaven that has the power to save, and that name is not yours.

Regardless of the mermaid on your tattoo.

PART TWO

WHAT A GOD!

Ponder the achievement of God.

He doesn't condone our sin, nor does he

compromise his standard.

He doesn't ignore our rebellion, nor does he relax

his demands.

Rather than dismiss our sin, he assumes our sin

and, incredibly, sentences himself.

God's holiness is honored. Our sin is punished . . .

and we are redeemed.

God does what we cannot do so we can be what we

dare not dream: perfect before God.

6 Calling the Corpses

Romans 3:21–26

All have turned away.
  Together, everyone has become useless.
There is no one who does good;
  there is not even one. . . .
This stops all excuses and brings the whole world
under God's judgment.   ROMANS 3:12, 19

A few weeks ago I traveled to the Midwest to pick up my two oldest daughters. They'd spent a week at camp. This wasn't their first time at camp, but it was their first time so far from home. The camp was great and the activities outstanding, but their hearts were heavy. They missed their mom and dad. And Mom and Dad weren't doing so well either.

Not wanting to risk any delayed flights, I flew up a day early. Parents weren't allowed to see their kids until 5:00 P.M., so I enjoyed the area, visited a few sights, and kept an eye on the time. My purpose wasn't to sightsee. My purpose was my kids.

I arrived at the camp at 3:00 P.M. A rope was stretched across the dirt road, and a sign dangling from the rope reminded me, "Parents may not enter until 5:00 P.M."

I wasn't alone at the rope. Other parents were already present. There was a lot of glancing at wristwatches. No in-depth conversations, just the expected, "How are you?" "Where are you from?" "And how many kids?" Nothing much beyond that. Our minds were down that dirt road. At about 4:30, I noticed a few dads positioning themselves near the rope. Not to be outdone, I did the same. Though most of the slots were taken, there was room for one more parent. I squeezed past one mother who was unaware that the horses had been called to the track. I felt sorry for her, but not enough to give her my spot.

With five minutes to go, conversation ended. No more playing games; this was serious stuff. The cars were on the track. The runners were in the blocks. The countdown was on. All we needed was someone to lower the rope.

Two camp counselors appeared to perform the honors. They knew better than to take one end of the rope and cross the road to allow the parents to enter. Such a move would have been fatal; they wouldn't have survived the stampede. Rather than endanger their lives, each took one end of the rope and, on a prearranged signal, lowered it to the ground. (They had done this before.)

We were off!

I was ready for this moment. I had waited long enough. I began with a brisk walk, but out of the corner of my eye I saw a dad starting to trot. *So that's what it's going to take, eh?* Good thing I was wearing jogging shoes. I broke into a run. Enough preliminaries. The hour had struck and the rope was down, and I was willing to do what it took to see my kids.

God feels the same.

God is ready to see his own. He, too, is separated from his children. He, too, will do whatever is necessary to take them home.

Yet, his desire leaves ours in the dust. Forget plane trips and rental cars; we're talking incarnation and sacrifice. Forget a night in a hotel; how about a lifetime on earth! I went from the state of Texas to the state of Missouri. He went from the state of being worshiped in heaven to being a baby in Bethlehem.

Why? He knows his children are without their father. And he knows we are powerless to return without his help.

Sin, the Universal Problem

But what separates us from God is not a rope and a camp policy. What separates us from God is sin. We aren't strong enough to remove it, and we aren't good enough to erase it. For all of our differences, there is one problem we all share. We are separated from God.

"There is *no one* who always does what is right, *not even one*. There is *no one* who understands. There is *no one* who looks to God for help. All have turned away. Together, everyone has become useless. There is *no one* who does anything good; there is *not even one*" (Rom. 3:10–11, italics mine).

Get the impression that Paul is trying to tell us something?

Every person on God's green earth has blown it. The hedonists blew it because they were pleasure-centered and not God-centered. The judgmentalists blew it because they were high-minded and not God-minded. The legalists blew it because they were work-driven and not grace-driven.

The hut-builders sought pleasure, the fault-finders sought impunity, the rock-stackers sought piety. The first disregards God, the second seeks to distract God, and the third hopes to reimburse God. But each one misses God. All are godless.

None are like the fourth son, who depended upon the father's plan to bring him home.

Death, the Universal Condition

This is the great shortfall of humanity. We're a long way from our Father and don't have a clue about how to get home.

Listen as Paul assumes the role of county coroner and describes the cadaver of the sinner.

"Their throats are like open graves."

"They use their tongues for telling lies."

"The poison of vipers is on their lips."

"Their mouths are full of cursing and hate."

"Their feet are swift to shed blood" (see Rom. 3:13, 14, 16).

What a repulsive anatomy! Throats like open graves. Deceitful tongues. Viper lips. Mouths full of vulgarity. Feet that march toward violence. And to sum it up, Paul presents the cause of it all, "There is no fear of God before their eyes" (v. 18 NIV).

Sin infects the entire person, from eyes to feet. Not only does sin contaminate every human being, it contaminates the being of every human. Paul will say it most clearly later in the letter to the Romans. "The wages of sin is death . . ." (6:23 NIV).

Sin is a fatal disease.

Sin has sentenced us to a slow, painful death.

Sin does to a life what shears do to a flower. A cut at the stem separates a flower from the source of life. Initially the flower is attractive, still colorful and strong. But watch that flower over a period of time, and the leaves will wilt and the petals will drop. No matter what you do, the flower will never live again. Surround it with water. Stick the stem in soil. Baptize it with fertilizer. Glue the flower back on the stem. Do what you wish. The flower is dead.

When the Chinese dictator Mao Zedong died in 1976, his physician, Dr. Li Zhisui, was given an impossible task. The Politburo demanded, "The chairman's body is to be permanently preserved." The staff objected. The doctor objected. He had seen the dry and shrunken remains of Lenin and Stalin. He knew a body with no life was doomed to rot.

But he had his commands. Twenty-two liters of formaldehyde were pumped into the body. The result was horrifying. Mao's face swelled up like a ball, and his neck was as thick as his head. His ears stuck out in right angles, and the chemical oozed from his pores. A team of embalmers worked for five hours with towels and cotton balls to force the liquids down into his body. Finally the face looked normal, but the chest was so swollen that his jacket had to be slit in the back and his body covered with the red Communist Party flag.

That sufficed for the funeral, but the powers above wanted the body permanently preserved to lie in state at Tiananmen Square. For a year Dr. Zhisui supervised a team working in an underground hospital as they tried to preserve the remains. Because of the futility of the task, a government official ordered that an identical wax dummy be made. Both the body and the replica were taken to the mausoleum in Tiananmen Square. Tens of thousands came to file past a crystal casket and pay their respects to the man who'd ruled China for twenty-seven years. But even the doctor didn't know if they were seeing Mao or a waxwork dummy.[1]

Don't we do the same? Isn't that the occupation of humanity? Isn't that the hope of the workaholic? Isn't that the aspiration of the greedy, the power-monger, and the adulterer? Not to pump formaldehyde into a corpse but to pump life into a soul?

We fool just enough people to keep ourselves trying a bit longer. Sometimes, even we don't know if people are seeing the real self or a wax figure.

A dead flower has no life.

A dead body has no life.

A dead soul has no life.

Cut off from God, the soul withers and dies. The consequence of sin is not a bad day or a bad mood but a dead soul. The sign of a dead soul is clear: poisoned lips and cursing mouths, feet that lead to violence and eyes that don't see God.

Now you know how people can be so vulgar. Their souls are dead. Now you see how some religions can be so oppressive. They have no life. Now you understand how the drug peddler can sleep at night and the dictator can live with his conscience. He has none.

The finished work of sin is to kill the soul.

We Need a Miracle

Upon seeing the problem, can't we see the solution? The solution is not more government or education, not more formaldehyde in the corpse. Nor is the solution more religion; man-made rituals and doctrines may seem to reattach the flower to the stem but they can't. We don't need more religion; we need a miracle. We don't need someone to disguise the dead; we need someone to raise the dead.

That "someone" is introduced in Romans 3:22.

But before we read the verse, I have to pause and warn you: Prepare yourself for its simplicity. No need to brew mystical concoctions. Elaborate ceremonies are unnecessary. Complicated treatments are unneeded. Tortuous hours of rehabilitation are not required. God's solution for our malady is starkly simple.

Before we read the verse, I also have to pause and ask: Aren't you glad the letter didn't stop with verses 19 and 20? "This stops all excuses and brings the whole world under God's judgment, because no one can be made right with God by following the law. The law only shows us our sin."

Aren't you relieved Paul didn't leave the corpse on the table? Aren't you happy that the apostle didn't describe the condition without showing God's solution? Don't worry. Of that there was no danger. A freight train couldn't have kept Paul from writing the next verse. These words are the ones he's been waiting to write. The next lines are the reason for the epistle, even his reason for living.

For sixty-one verses we have sat with Paul in a darkened room as he described the fatality of sin. Every candle is down to the wick. Every lamp is empty of oil. There is a hearth, but it has no wood. There is a lantern, but it has no flame. We have groped in every corner and found no light. Unable to see even our hand before our faces, all we can do is stare into the night. We are unaware that Paul has crept next to a window and placed his hand on the latch. Just when we wonder if there is any light to be found, Paul throws open the shutters and announces: "But God has a way!" (v. 21).

> But God has a way to make people right with him without the law, and he has now shown us that way. . . . God makes people right with himself through their faith in Jesus Christ. This is true for all who believe in Christ, because all people are the same: All have sinned and are not good enough for God's glory, and all need to be made right with God by his grace, which is a free gift. They need to be made free from sin through Jesus Christ. God gave him as a way to forgive sin through faith in the blood of Jesus' death. This showed that God always does what is right and fair, as in the past when he was patient and did not punish people for their sins. (vv. 21–25)

Man's Windfall

As youngsters, we neighborhood kids would play street football. The minute we got home from school, we'd drop the books and hit the pavement. The kid across the street had a dad with a great arm and a strong addiction to football. As soon as he'd pull in the driveway from work we'd start yelling for him to come and play ball. He couldn't resist. Out of fairness he'd always ask, "Which team is losing?" Then he would join that team, which often seemed to be mine.

His appearance in the huddle changed the whole ball game. He was confident, strong, and most of all, he had a plan. We'd circle around him, and he'd look at us and say, "OK boys, here is what we are going to do." The other side was groaning before we left the huddle. You see, we not only had a new plan, we had a new leader.

He brought new life to our team. God does precisely the same. We didn't need a new play; we needed a new plan. We didn't need to trade positions; we needed a new player. That player is Jesus Christ, God's firstborn son.

"Though we were spiritually dead because of the things we did against God, he gave us new life with Christ" (Eph. 2:5). God's solution is not to preserve the dead—but to raise the dead. "Therefore, if anyone is in Christ, he is a new creation; the old has gone; the new has come!" (2 Cor. 5:17 NIV).

What Jesus did with Lazarus, he is willing to do with us. Which is good to know, for what Martha said about Lazarus can be said about us, "But, Lord, it has been four days since he died. There will be a bad smell" (John 11:39). Martha was speaking for us all. The human race is dead, and there is a bad smell. We have been dead and buried a long time. We don't need someone to fix us up; we need someone to raise us up. In the muck and mire of what we call life, there is death, and we have been in it so long we've grown accustomed to the stink. But Christ hasn't.

And Christ can't stand the thought of his kids rotting in the cemetery. So he comes in and calls us out. We are the corpse, and he is the corpse-caller. We are the dead, and he is the dead-raiser.

Our task is not to get up but to admit we are dead. The only ones who remain in the grave are the ones who don't think they are there.

The stone has been moved. "Lazarus!" he yells. "Larry! Sue! Horatio! Come out!" He calls.

"Andrea! Jenna! I'm here!" I shouted as I ran down the camp road. (I won the race.) I spotted Andrea first. She was under a canopy preparing to practice gymnastics. I called her name again. "Daddy!" she yelled and jumped into my arms.

There was no guarantee she'd respond. Though I had flown a thousand miles, rented a car, and waited an hour, she could have seen me and—heaven forbid!—ignored me. Some kids are too grown up to run to their parent in front of their friends.

But then there are those who have had enough camp food and mosquito repellent to make them jump for joy at the sight of their father. Such was the case with Andrea.

All of a sudden, Andrea had gone from feeling homesick to feeling happy. Why? Only one difference. Her father had come to take her home.

Where Love and Justice Meet

God has a way to make people right with him without the law, and he has now shown us that way which the law and the prophets told us about. God makes people right with himself through their faith in Jesus Christ. ROMANS 3:21–22

I'm glad the letter wasn't sent from heaven. It came from my automobile insurance company, my *former* automobile insurance company. I didn't drop them; they dropped me. Not because I didn't pay my premiums; I was on time and caught up. Not because I failed to do the paperwork; every document was signed and delivered.

I was dropped for making too many mistakes.

The letter begins by politely telling me that my record has been under review.

We have secured Motor Vehicle Records which indicate a speed violation by Max Lucado in December and January and a not-at-fault accident by Denalyn Lucado in December. Additional records indicate additional speed violations by Mr. Lucado in April and by Mrs. Lucado in December of the next year.

Now, I'm the first to admit that Denalyn and I tend to get a bit heavy-footed and careless. In fact, that is the reason we have insurance. Aren't the blemishes on my record an indication that I am a worthy client? Wasn't the whole insurance business invented for people like me? Don't my fender-benders and bumps put food on some adjuster's table? If not for my blunders, what would the actuaries actuate?

My initial thought was that the company was writing to congratulate me on being a good customer. *Maybe they're writing to invite me to a banquet or to tell me I've won an award,* I thought.

The letter continued, documenting other secrets of our past:

Our records indicate that on November 18 we paid to fix damage to another vehicle when Max Lucado backed into another car in a parking lot.

The twofold appearance of the word *another* alarmed me. "Another" vehicle. "Another" car. Somebody is counting! Perhaps I need to urge them to read 1 Corinthians 13:5, "Love . . . keeps no record of wrongs" (NIV). The letter continued with another set of "anothers".

In April we paid to fix another vehicle when Denalyn Lucado hit the rear of another car at a stop sign.

"But she was giving the baby a bottle!" I said in her defense to no one listening. Denalyn was at a stoplight. Sara dropped her bottle in the floorboard and was crying, so Denalyn leaned over and picked it up and bumped the car ahead of her. Honest mistake. Could have happened to anyone.

And that time I backed into another car? I reported it! I was the one who walked into the building, found the owner, and told him what I had done. Confessed my fault. I did my part. I could have backed into the car and driven off, which, to be honest, I did consider but didn't do. Should I also share with them 1 John 1:9? "If we confess our sins, he will forgive our sins . . ."

Don't I get some credit for being honest?

Apparently not. Read the conclusion of the letter.

In view of the above information, we are not willing to reinstate your automobile insurance policy. The policy will terminate at 12:01 A.M. Standard Time January 4. I'm sorry our reply could not have been more favorable. For your protection, you are urged to obtain other insurance to prevent any lapse in coverage.

Wait a minute. Let me see if I get this right. I bought insurance to cover my mistakes. But then I get dropped for making mistakes. Hello. Did I miss something? Did I fail to see a footnote? Did I skip some fine print in the contract?

Did I overlook a paragraph that read, "We, the aforesaid company will consider one Max Lucado insurable until he shows himself to be one who needs insurance upon which time his coverage ceases"?

Isn't that like a doctor treating healthy patients only? Or a dentist hanging a sign in the window, "No cavities, please"? Or a teacher penalizing you for asking too many questions? Isn't that like qualifying for a loan by proving you don't need one? What if the fire department said it would protect you *until* you had a fire? What if a bodyguard said he'd protect you *unless* someone was after you? Or a lifeguard said she'd watch over you unless you started to drown?

Or what if, perish the thought, heaven had limitations to its coverage? What if you got a letter from the Pearly Gate Underwriting Division that read:

Dear Mrs. Smith,

> *I'm writing in response to this morning's request for forgiveness. I'm sorry to inform you that you have reached your quota of sins. Our records show that, since employing our services, you have erred seven times in the area of greed, and your prayer life is substandard when compared to others of like age and circumstance.*

> *Further review reveals that your understanding of doctrine is in the lower 20 percentile and you have excessive tendencies to gossip. Because of your sins you are a high-risk candidate for heaven. You understand that grace has its limits. Jesus sends his regrets and kindest regards and hopes that you will find some other form of coverage.*

Many fear receiving such a letter. Some worry they already have! If an insurance company can't cover my honest mistakes, can I expect God to cover my intentional rebellion?

Paul answers the question with what John Stott calls "the most startling statement in Romans."[1] God "makes even evil people right in his sight" (Rom. 4:5). What an incredible claim! It's one thing to make good people right, but those who are evil? We can expect God to justify the decent, but the dirty? Surely coverage is provided for the driver with the clean record, but the speeder? The ticketed? The high-risk client? How in the world can justification come for the evil?

The Direction of Grace

It can't. It can't come from the world. It must come from heaven. Man has no way, but *God has a way* . . .

Up until this point in Paul's letter all efforts at salvation have been from earth upward. Man has inflated his balloon with his own hot air and not been able to leave the atmosphere. Our pleas of ignorance are inexcusable (Rom. 1:20). Our comparisons with others are impermissible (2:1). Our religious merits are unacceptable

(2:29). The conclusion is unavoidable: self-salvation simply does not work. Man has no way to save himself.

But Paul announces that *God has a way*. Where man fails God excels. Salvation comes from heaven downward, not earth upward. "A new day *from* heaven will dawn upon us" (Luke 1:78). "Every good action and every perfect gift is *from* God" (James 1:17).

Please note: Salvation is God-given, God-driven, God-empowered, and God-originated. The gift is not from man to God. It is from God to man. "It is not our love for God; it is God's love for us in sending his Son to be the way to take away our sins" (1 John 4:10).

Grace is created by God and given to man. "Sky above, make victory fall like rain; clouds, pour down victory. Let the earth receive it, and let salvation grow, and let victory grow with it. I, the LORD, have created it" (Isa. 45:8).

On the basis of this point alone, Christianity is set apart from any other religion in the world. "No other system, ideology or religion proclaims a free forgiveness and a new life to those who have done nothing to deserve it but deserve judgment instead."[2]

To quote John MacArthur: "As far as the way of salvation is concerned, there are only two religions the world has ever known or will ever know—the religion of divine accomplishment, which is biblical Christianity, and the religion of human achievement, which includes all other kinds of religion, by whatever names they may go under."[3]

Every other approach to God is a bartering system; if I do this, God will do that. I'm either saved by works (what I do), emotions (what I experience), or knowledge (what I know).

By contrast, Christianity has no whiff of negotiation at all. Man is not the negotiator; indeed, man has no grounds from which to negotiate.

Those closest to God have understood this. Those nearest to

him have never boasted about their deeds; in fact, they were most disgusted by the thought of self-salvation. They describe legalism in repulsive terms. Isaiah said our righteous acts are "like filthy pieces of cloth," referring to menstrual cloth (Isa. 64:6). Paul equated our religious credentials with the pile of stink you avoid in the cow pasture. ("[I] do count them but dung" [Phil. 3:8 KJV]).

We can summarize the first three and one-half chapters of Romans with three words: *We have failed.*

We have attempted to reach the moon but scarcely made it off the ground. We tried to swim the Atlantic, but couldn't get beyond the reef. We have attempted to scale the Everest of salvation, but we have yet to leave the base camp, much less ascend the slope. The quest is simply too great; we don't need more supplies or muscle or technique; we need a helicopter.

Can't you hear it hovering?

"God has a way to *make people right with him*" (Rom. 3:21, italics mine). How vital that we embrace this truth. God's highest dream is not to make us rich, not to make us successful or popular or famous. God's dream is to make us right with him.

The Dilemma of Grace

How does God make us right with him? Let's return to the insurance company and ask a few questions: First, was it unjust in dismissing me as a client? No. I may find its decision distasteful, unenjoyable, even disheartening, but I cannot call it unfair. It only did what it said it would do.

So did our Father. He told Adam, "If you ever eat fruit from that tree, you will die" (Gen. 2:17). No fine print. No hidden agenda. No loophole or technicality. God has not played games with us. He has been fair. Since Eden, the wages of sin have been death (Rom. 6:23).

Just as reckless driving has its consequences, so does reckless living. Just as I have no defense before the insurance company, I have no defense before God. My record accuses me. My past convicts me.

Now, suppose the founder and CEO of the insurance company chose to have mercy upon me. Suppose, for some reason, he wanted to keep me as a client. What can he do? Can't he just close his eyes and pretend I made no mistakes? Why doesn't he take my driving record and tear it up? Two reasons.

First, the integrity of the company would be compromised. He would have to relax the standards of the organization, something he could not and should not do. The ideals of the organization are too valuable to be abandoned. The company cannot abandon its precepts and still maintain integrity.

Second, the mistakes of the driver would be encouraged. If there is no price for my mistakes, why should I drive carefully? If the president will dismiss my errors, then what's to keep me from driving however I want? If he is willing to ignore any blunders, then blunder on!

Is that the aim of the president? Is that the goal of his mercy? Lowered standards and poor driving? No. The president is faced with this dilemma. *How can I be merciful and fair at the same time? How can I offer grace without endorsing mistakes?*

Or, put in biblical terms, how can God punish the sin and love the sinner? Paul has made it clear, "The wrath of God is being revealed from heaven against all godlessness and wickedness" (Rom. 1:18 NIV). Is God going to lower his standard so we can be forgiven? Is God going to look away and pretend I've never sinned? Would we want a God who altered the rules and made exceptions? No. We want a God who "does not change like . . . shifting shadows" (James 1:17) and who "judges all people in the same way" (Rom. 2:11).

Besides, to ignore my sin is to endorse my sin. If my sin has no price, then sin on! If my sin brings no pain, then sin on! In fact, "We should do evil so that good will come" (Rom. 3:8). Is this the aim of God? To compromise his holiness and enable our evil?

Of course not. Then what is he to do? How can he be just and love the sinner? How can he be loving and punish the sin? How can he satisfy his standard *and* forgive my mistakes? Is there any way God could honor the integrity of heaven without turning his back on me?

The Decision of Grace

Holiness demands that sin be punished. Mercy compels that the sinner be loved. How can God do both? May I answer the question by returning to the insurance executive? Imagine him inviting me to his office and saying these words.

"Mr. Lucado, I have found a way to deal with your mistakes. I can't overlook them; to do so would be unjust. I can't pretend you didn't commit them; to do so would be a lie. But here is what I can do. In our records we have found a person with a spotless past. He has never broken a law. Not one violation, not one trespass, not even a parking ticket. He has volunteered to trade records with you. We will take your name and put it on his record. We will take his name and put it on yours. We will punish him for what you did. You, who did wrong, will be made right. He, who did right, will be made wrong."

My response? "You've got to be kidding! Who would do this for me? Who is this person?"

To which the president answers, "Me."

If you're waiting for an insurance executive to say that, don't hold your breath. He won't. He can't. Even if he wanted to he couldn't. He has no perfect record.

But if you're wanting God to say those words, you can sigh with relief. He has. He can. For "God was in Christ, making peace between the world and himself. . . . Christ had no sin, but God made him become sin so that in Christ we could become right with God" (2 Cor. 5:19, 21).

The perfect record of Jesus was given to you, and your imperfect record was given to Christ. Jesus was "not guilty, but he suffered for those who are guilty to bring you to God" (1 Peter 3:18). As a result, God's holiness is honored and his children are forgiven.

By his perfect life Jesus fulfilled the commands of the law. By his death he satisfied the demands of sin. Jesus suffered not like a sin-ner, but as a sinner. Why else would he cry, "My God, my God, why have You forsaken Me?" (Matt. 27:46 NKJV).

Ponder the achievement of God. He doesn't condone our sin; nor does he compromise his standard. He doesn't ignore our rebel-lion; nor does he relax his demands. Rather than dismiss our sin he assumes our sin and, incredibly, sentences himself. God's holiness is honored. Our sin is punished. And we are redeemed. God is still God. The wages of sin is still death. And we are made perfect.

That's right, *perfect*. "With one sacrifice he made perfect forever those who are being made holy" (Heb. 10:14).

God justifies (makes perfect) then sanctifies (makes holy). God does what we cannot do so we can be what we dare not dream, per-fect before God. He justly justifies the unjust.

And what did he do with your poor driving record? "He can-celed the debt, which listed all the rules we failed to follow. He took away that record with its rules and nailed it to the cross" (Col. 2:14).

And what should be your response? Let's go one more time to the insurance company. I return to my agent and ask him to call up my file. He does and stares at the computer screen in disbelief. "Mr. Lucado, you have a perfect past. Your performance is spotless."

My response? If I'm dishonest and ungrateful, I will deepen my voice and cross my arms and say, "You are right. It's not easy to be great."

If I'm honest and grateful, I will simply smile and say, "I don't deserve that compliment. In fact, I don't deserve that record. It was and is an unspeakable gift of grace."

By the way, I have a new automobile-insurance company. They charge me a little more since I've been bumped from a competitor. And who knows? I may get a few more letters before it's all over.

My eternal soul is under heavenly coverage, and Jesus isn't known for dismissing clients. He is known, however, for paying premiums and I'm paid up for life. I'm in good hands with him.

Before moving to the next chapter, let me field a question. There's a fellow who's had his hand up ever since the last paragraph on page 74. Yes sir? You're finding this all too . . . what?

I'm sorry, I still didn't understand . . . too good to be what? Too good to be *true*? Ah . . . well. You're not the first. In fact, Paul knew many of us would question the issue. That's why he wrote Romans 4. That's why I wrote the next chapter.

Excuse me? You have another question? Yes, you do look familiar. You sold me what? The insurance policy? The one you later canceled? Hmmm. I bet you do have a hard time understanding grace.

8 | Credit Where Credit Is Not Due

Romans 3:27–4:25

A person is made right with God through faith, not through obeying the law. ROMANS 3:28

Remember the good ol' days when credit cards were imprinted by hand? The clerk would take your plastic and place it in the imprint machine, and *rrack-rrack*, the numbers would be registered and the purchase would be made. I learned to operate such a device in a gasoline station on the corner of Broadway and Fourth when I was fourteen years old. For a dollar an hour I cleaned windshields, pumped gas, and checked the oil. (Yes, Virginia, gas-station attendants did those things back then.)

My favorite task, however, was imprinting credit cards. There's nothing like the surge of power you feel when you run the imprinter over the plastic. I'd always steal a glance at the customer to watch him wince as I *rrack-rracked* his card.

Credit-card purchases today aren't nearly as dramatic. Nowadays the magnetic strip is swiped through the slot, or the numbers are entered on the keyboard. No noise. No drama. No pain. Bring back the *rrack-rrack* days when the purchase was announced for all to hear.

You buy gas, *rrack-rrack*.

You charge some clothes, *rrack-rrack*.

You pay for dinner, *rrack-rrack*.

If the noise didn't get you, the statement at the end of the month would. Thirty days is ample time to *rrack* up enough purchases to *rrack* your budget.

And a lifetime is enough to *rrack* up some major debt in heaven.

You yell at your kids, *rrack-rrack*.

You covet a friend's car, *rrack-rrack*.

You envy your neighbor's success, *rrack-rrack*.

You break a promise, *rrack-rrack*.

You lie, *rrack-rrack*.

You lose control, *rrack-rrack*.

You doze off reading this book, *rrack-rrack*, *rrack-rrack*, *rrack-rrack*.

Further and further in debt.

Initially, we attempt to repay what we owe. (Remember the rock-stacker?) Every prayer is a check written, and each good deed is a payment made. If we can do one good act for every bad act, then won't our account balance out in the end? If I can counter my cussing with compliments, my lusts with loyalties, my complaints with contributions, my vices with victories—then won't my account be justified?

It would, except for two problems.

First, I don't know the *cost* of each sin. The price of gas is easy to find. Would that it were so clear with sin. It's not. What, for example, is the charge for getting mad in traffic? I get ticked off at some fellow who cuts in front of me, what do I do to pay for my crime? Drive fifty in a fifty-five zone? Give a wave and a smile to ten consecutive cars? Who knows? Or what if I wake up in a bad mood? What's the charge for a couple of mopey hours? Will one church service next Sunday offset one grumpy morning today? And what qualifies for a bad mood? Is the charge for grumpiness less on cloudy days than clear? Or am I permitted a certain number of grouchy days per year?

This can get confusing, you know.

And not only don't I know the cost of my sins, I don't always know the *occasion* of my sins. There are times when I sin and I don't even know it! I was twelve years old before I realized it was a sin to hate your enemy. My bike was stolen when I was eight. I hated the thief for four years! How do I pay for those sins? Do I get an exemption based on ignorance?

And what about the sins I'm committing now without realizing it? What if somebody somewhere discovers it is a sin to play golf? Or what if God thinks the way I play golf is a sin? Oh, boy. I'll have some serious settling up to do.

And what about our secret sins? Even as I write this chapter, I'm sinning. I'd like to think I'm writing to the glory of God, but am I? Am I free of vanity? Does this vessel have only concern for contents and no concern for the container? Hardly. I wonder if people will agree, if they'll approve, if they'll appreciate all the long, painstaking, tedious, exhausting, tortuous hours I am humbly putting into these watershed, historic thoughts.

And what of you? Any sins of omission on this month's statement? Did you miss any chance to do good? Overlook an opportunity to forgive? Neglect an open door to serve? Did you seize *every* chance to encourage your friends?

Rrack-rrack, rrack-rrack, rrack-rrack.

And there are other concerns. The grace period, for example.

My credit card allows a minimal payment and then rolls the debt into the next month. Does God? Will he let me pay off today's greed next year? What about interest? If I leave a sin on my statement for several months, does it incur more sin? And speaking of the statement . . . where is it? Can I see it? Who has it? How do I pay the blasted thing off?

There it is. That's the question. How do I deal with the debt I owe to God?

Deny it? My conscience won't let me.

Find worse sins in others? God won't fall for that.

Claim lineage immunity? Family pride won't help.

Try to pay it off? I could, but that takes us back to the problem. We don't know the cost of sin. We don't even know how much we owe.

Then what do we do? Listen to Paul's answer in what one scholar says is "possibly the most important single paragraph ever written."[1]

> All need to be made right with God by his grace, which is a free gift. They need to be made free from sin through Jesus Christ. God gave him as a way to forgive sin through faith in the blood of Jesus. (Rom. 3:24–25)

Simply put: The cost of your sins is more than you can pay. The gift of your God is more than you can imagine. "A person is made right with God through faith," Paul explains, "not through obeying the law" (v. 28).

This may very well be the most difficult spiritual truth for us to embrace. For some reason, people accept Jesus as Lord before they accept him as Savior. It's easier to comprehend his power than his mercy. We'll celebrate the empty tomb long before we'll kneel at the cross. We, like Thomas, would die for Christ before we'd let Christ die for us.

We aren't alone. We aren't the first to struggle with Paul's presentation of grace. Apparently, the first ones to doubt the epistle to the Romans were the first to read it. In fact, you get the impression Paul can hear their questions. The apostle lifts his pen from the page and imagines his readers: some squirming, some doubting, some denying. Anticipating their thoughts, he deals with their objections.

Objection #1: Too Risky to Be True

The first objection comes from the pragmatist. "Do we destroy the law by following the way of faith?" (Rom. 3:31). The concern here is motivation. "If I'm not saved by my works, then why work? If I'm not saved by the law, then why keep the law? If I'm not saved by what I do, then why do anything?"

You've got to admit grace is risky. There *is* the chance that people will take it to an extreme. There *is* the possibility that people will abuse God's goodness.

A further word about credit cards might be helpful here. My father had a simple rule about them: Own as few as possible and pay them off as soon as possible. His salary as a mechanic was sufficient but not abundant, and he hated the thought of paying interest. He made it a point to pay the balance in full at the end of the month. You can imagine my surprise when he put a credit card in my hand the day I left for college.

Standing in the driveway with car packed and farewells said, he handed it to me. I looked at the name on the plastic; it wasn't mine, it was his. He had ordered an extra card for me. His only instructions to me were, "Be careful how you use it."

Pretty risky, don't you think? As I was driving to college it occurred to me that I was a free man. I could go anywhere I wanted to go. I had wheels and a tank of gas. I had my clothes. I had money in my pocket and a stereo in the trunk and, most of all, I had a credit card. I was a slave set free! The chains were off. I could be in Mexico before nightfall! What was to keep me from going wild?

Such is the question of the pragmatist. What is to keep us from going wild? If worshiping doesn't save me, why worship? If tithing doesn't save me, why give? If my morality doesn't save me, then watch out, ladies, here I come! Jude warns of this attitude when he speaks of people who "abuse his grace as an opportunity for immorality" (Jude 4 PHILLIPS).

Later Paul will counter his critics with the question, "So do you think we should continue sinning so that God will give us even more grace! No!" (Rom. 6:1). Or as one translator writes, "What a ghastly thought!" (PHILLIPS).

A ghastly thought, indeed. Grace promoting evil? Mercy endorsing sin? What a horrible idea! The apostle uses the strongest Greek idiom possible to repudiate the idea: *Me genoito!* The phrase literally means "may it never be!" As he has already said, God's "kindness is meant to lead you to repentance" (Rom. 2:4 TLB).

Get it straight: Someone who sees grace as permission to sin has missed grace entirely. Mercy understood is holiness desired. "[Jesus] gave himself for us so he might pay the price to free us from all evil and to make us pure people who belong only to him—*people who are always wanting to do good deeds*" (Titus 2:14, italics mine).

Note that last phrase: "people who are always wanting to do good deeds." Grace fosters an eagerness for good. Grace doesn't spawn a desire to sin. If one has truly embraced God's gift, he will not mock it. In fact, if a person uses God's mercy as liberty to sin, one might wonder whether the person ever knew God's mercy at all.

When my father gave me his card, he didn't attach a list of regulations. There was no contract for me to sign or rules for me to read. He didn't tell me to place my hand on the Bible and pledge to reimburse him for any expenses. In fact, he didn't ask for any payment at all. As things turned out, I went a few weeks into the semester without using it. Why? Because he gave me more than a card; he gave me his trust. And where I might break his rules, I wasn't about to abuse his trust.

God's trust makes us eager to do right. Such is the genius of grace. The law can show us where we do wrong, but it can't make us eager to do right. Grace can. Or as Paul answers, "Faith causes us to be what the law truly wants" (Rom. 3:31).

Objection #2: Too New to Be True

The second objection to grace comes from a man who is cautious of anything new. "Don't give me any of this newfangled teaching. Just give me the law. If it was good enough for Abraham, it is good enough for me."

"All right, let me tell you about the faith of your father, Abraham," Paul answers.

"If Abraham was made right by the things he did, he had a reason to brag. But this is not God's view, because the Scripture says, 'Abraham believed God, and God accepted Abraham's faith, and that faith made him right with God'" (4:2–3).

These words must have stunned the Jews. Paul points to Abraham as a prototype of grace. The Jews upheld Abraham as a man who was blessed *because* of his obedience. Not the case, argues Paul. The first book in the Bible says that Abraham "believed the Lord, and he credited it to him as righteousness" (Gen. 15:6 NIV). It was his faith, not his works, that made him right with God. *The Message* renders Romans 4:2, "[Abraham] trusted God to set him right instead of trying to be right on his own."

Five times in six verses Paul uses the word *credit*. The term is common in the financial world. To credit an account is to make a deposit. If I credit your account then I either increase your balance or lower your debt.

Wouldn't it be nice if someone credited your charge-card account? All month long you *rrack-rrack* up the bills, dreading the day the statement comes in the mail. When it comes you leave it on your desk for a few days, not wanting to see how much you owe. Finally, you force yourself to open the envelope. With one eye closed and the other open, you peek at the number. What you read causes the other eye to pop open. "A zero balance!"

There must be a mistake, so you call the bank that issued the card. "Yes," the bank manager explains, "your account is paid in full. A Mr. Max Lucado sent us a check to cover your debt."

You can't believe your ears. "How do you know his check is good?"

"Oh, there is no doubt. Mr. Lucado has been paying off people's debts for years."

By the way, I'd love to do that for you, but don't get your hopes up. I have a few bills of my own. But Jesus would love to, and he can! He has no personal debt at all. And, what's more, he has been doing it for years. For proof Paul reaches into the two-thousand-year-old file marked "Abram of Ur" and pulls out a statement. The statement has its share of charges. Abram was far from perfect. There were times when he trusted the Egyptians before he trusted God. He even lied, telling Pharaoh that his wife was his sister. But Abram made one decision that changed his eternal life: "He trusted God to set him right instead of trying to be right on his own" (Rom. 4:3 MSG).

Here is a man justified by faith before his circumcision (v. 10), before the law (v. 13), before Moses and the Ten Commandments. Here is a man justified by faith before the cross! The sin-covering blood of Calvary extends as far into the past as it does into the future.

Abraham is not the only Old Testament hero to cast himself

upon God's grace. "David said the same thing. He said that people are truly blessed when God, without paying attention to good deeds, makes people right with himself. 'Happy are they whose sins are forgiven, whose wrongs are pardoned. Happy is the person whom God does not consider guilty'" (vv. 6–8).

We must not see grace as a provision made after the law had failed. Grace was offered *before* the law was revealed. Indeed, grace was offered before man was created! "You were bought, not with something that ruins like gold or silver, but with the precious blood of Christ, who was like a pure and perfect lamb. Christ was chosen before the world was made, but he was shown to the world in these last times for your sake" (1 Pet. 1:18–20).

Why would God offer grace before we needed it? Glad you asked. Let's return one final time to the charge card my father gave me. Did I mention that I went several months without needing it? But when I needed it, I *really* needed it. You see, I wanted to visit a friend on another campus. Actually, the friend was a girl in another city, six hours away. On an impulse I skipped class one Friday morning and headed out. Not knowing whether my parents would approve, I didn't ask their permission. Because I left in a hurry, I forgot to take any money. I made the trip without their knowledge and with an empty wallet.

Everything went fine until I rear-ended a car on the return trip. Using a crowbar, I pried the fender off my front wheel so the car could limp to a gas station. I can still envision the outdoor phone where I stood in the autumn chill. My father, who assumed I was on campus, took my collect call and heard my tale. My story wasn't much to boast about. I'd made a trip without his knowledge, without any money, and wrecked his car.

"Well," he said after a long pause, "these things happen. That's why I gave you the card. I hope you learned a lesson."

Did I learn a lesson? I certainly did. I learned that my father's forgiveness predated my mistake. He had given me the card before my wreck in the event that I would have one. He had provided for my blunder before I blundered. Need I tell you that God has done the same? Please understand, Dad didn't want me to wreck the car. He didn't give me the card *so* that I would wreck the car. But he knew his son. And he knew his son would someday need grace.

Please understand, God doesn't want us to sin. He didn't give us grace *so* we would sin. But he knows his children. "He made their hearts and understands everything they do" (Ps. 33:15). "He knows how we were made" (Ps. 103:14). And he knew that we would someday need his grace.

Grace is nothing new. God's mercy predates Paul and his readers, predates David and Abraham; it even predates creation. It certainly predates any sin you've committed. God's grace is older than your sin and greater than your sin. Too good to be true? That's the third objection.

Objection #3: Too Good to Be True

Just as there was a pragmatist who said grace is too risky and a traditionalist who said grace is too new, there was likely a skeptic who said, "This is too good to be true."

This is by far the most common objection to grace. No one came into my office this week to ask me about Abraham and works and law and faith. But these walls did hear the question of the young woman who spent two university years saying yes to the flesh and no to God. I did talk to a young husband who wonders if God could forgive an abortion he funded a decade ago. There was the father who'd just realized he'd devoted his life to work and neglected his kids.

All are wondering if they've overextended their credit line with

God. They aren't alone. The vast majority of people simply state, "God may give grace to you, but not to me. You see, I've charted the waters of failure. I've pushed the envelope too many times. I'm not your typical sinner, I'm guilty of _____." And they fill in the blank.

How would you fill in the blank? Is there a chapter in your biography that condemns you? A valley of your heart too deep for the firstborn Son to reach? If you think there is no hope for you, then Paul has a person he wants you to meet. Our barren past reminds the apostle of Sarah's barren womb.

God had promised Sarah and Abram a child. In fact, the name Abram meant "exalted father." God even changed Abram's name to Abraham (father of many) but still no son. Forty years passed before the promise was honored. Don't you think the conversation became dreadfully routine for Abraham?

"What is your name?"

"Abraham."

"Oh, 'father of many'! What a great title. Tell me, how many sons do you have?"

Abraham would sigh and answer, "None."

God had promised a child, but Abraham had no son. He left his home for an unknown land, but no son was born. He overcame famine, but still had no son. His nephew Lot came and went, but still no son. He would have encounters with angels and Melchizedek, but still be without an heir.

By now Abraham was ninety-nine, and Sarah was not much younger. She knitted and he played solitaire, and both chuckled at the thought of bouncing a boy on their bony knees. He lost his hair, she lost her teeth, and neither spent a lot of time lusting for the other. But somehow they never lost hope. Occasionally, he'd think of God's promise and give her a wink, and she'd give him a smile and think, *Well, God did promise us a child, didn't he?*

When everything was hopeless, Abraham believed anyway, deciding to live not on the basis of what he saw he *couldn't* do, but on what God said he *would do*. . . .

Abraham didn't focus on his own impotence and say, "It's hopeless. This hundred-year-old body could never have a child." Nor did he survey Sarah's decades of infertility and give up. He didn't tiptoe around God's promise cautiously asking skeptical questions. He plunged into the promise and came up strong, ready for God. That's why it is said, "Abraham was declared fit before God by trusting God to set him right." (Rom. 4:18–21 MSG)

Everything was gone. No youth. No vigor. No strength. The get-up-and-go had got up and gone. All old Abe and Sarah had was a social-security check and a promise from heaven. But Abraham decided to trust the promise rather than focus on the problems. As a result the Medicare couple were the first to bring a crib into the nursing home.

Do we have much more than they? Not really. There's not a one of us who hasn't *rrack-rracked* up more bills than we could ever pay. But there's not a one of us who must remain in debt. The same God who gave a child to Abraham has promised grace to us.

What's more incredible, Sarah telling Abraham that he was a daddy, or God calling you and me righteous? Both are absurd. Both are too good to be true. But both are from God.

9 Major League Grace

Romans 5:1–3

Since we have been made right with God by our faith, we have peace with God. This happened through our Lord Jesus Christ, who has brought us into that blessing of God's grace that we now enjoy. We are happy because of the hope we have of sharing God's glory. ROMANS 5:1–2

Batters hustling to the plate to take their swings? Questionable calls going uncontested? Umpires being thanked after the game? Fans returning foul balls?

This is Major League Baseball?

It was. For a few weeks during the spring of '95, professional baseball was a different game. The million-dollar arms were at home. The Cadillac bats were in the rack. The contracted players were negotiating for more money. The owners, determined to start the season, threw open the gates to almost anybody who knew how to scoop a grounder or run out a bunt.

These weren't minor-leaguers. The minor leagues were also on strike. These were fellows who went from coaching Little League one week to wearing a Red Sox uniform the next.

The games weren't fancy, mind you. Line drives rarely reached the outfield. One manager said his pitchers threw the ball so slowly the radar gun couldn't clock them. A fan could shell a dozen peanuts in the time it took to relay a throw from the outfield. The players huffed and puffed more than the "Little Engine That Could."

But, my, did the players have fun! The diamond was studded with guys who played the game for the love of the game. When the coach said run, they ran. When he needed a volunteer to shag flies, a dozen hands went up. They arrived before the park was open, greasing their gloves and cleaning their cleats. When it was time to go home they stayed until the grounds crew ran them off. They thanked the attendants for washing their uniforms. They thanked the caterers for the food. They thanked the fans for paying the dollar to watch. The line of players willing to sign autographs was longer than the line of fans wanting them.

These guys didn't see themselves as a blessing to baseball but baseball as a blessing to them. They didn't expect luxury; they were surprised by it. They didn't demand more playtime; they were thrilled to play at all.

It was baseball again!

In Cincinnati the general manager stepped out on the field and applauded the fans for coming out. The Phillies gave away free hot dogs and sodas. In the trade of the year, the Cleveland Indians gave five players to the Cincinnati Reds—for free!

It wasn't classy. You missed the three-run homers and frozen-rope pick-offs. But that was forgiven for the pure joy of seeing some guys play who really enjoyed the game. What made them so special? Simple. They were living a life they didn't deserve. These guys didn't make it to the big leagues on skill; they made it on luck. They weren't picked because they were good; they were picked because they were willing.

And they knew it! Not one time did you read an article about the replacement players arguing over poor pay. I did read a story about a fellow who offered a hundred grand if some owner would sign him. There was no jockeying for position. No second-guessing the management. No strikes. No lockouts or walkouts. Heavens, these guys didn't even complain that their names weren't stitched on the jerseys. They were just happy to be on the team.

Shouldn't we be, as well? Aren't we a lot like these players? If the first four chapters of Romans tell us anything, they tell us we are living a life we don't deserve. We aren't good enough to get picked, but look at us, suited up and ready to play! We aren't skillful enough to make the community softball league, but our names are on the greatest roster of history!

Do we deserve to be here? No. But would we trade the privilege? Not for the world. For if Paul's proclamation is true, God's grace has placed us on a dream team beyond imagination. Our past is pardoned, and our future secure. And lest we forget this unspeakable gift, Paul itemizes the blessings that God's grace brings into our world (see Rom. 5:1–12).

Blessing #1: We Have Peace with God

"Since we have been made right with God by our faith, we have peace with God" (v. 1).

Peace with God. What a happy consequence of faith! Not just peace between countries, peace between neighbors, or peace at home; salvation brings peace with God.

Once a monk and his apprentice traveled from the abbey to a nearby village. The two parted at the city gates, agreeing to meet the next morning after completing their tasks. According to plan, they met and began the long walk back to the abbey. The monk noticed that the younger man was unusually quiet. He asked him if anything was wrong. "What business is it of yours?" came the terse response.

Now the monk was sure his brother was troubled, but he said nothing. The distance between the two began to increase. The apprentice walked slowly, as if to separate himself from his teacher. When the abbey came in sight, the monk stopped at the gate and waited on the student. "Tell me, my son. What troubles your soul?"

The boy started to react again, but when he saw the warmth in his master's eyes, his heart began to melt. "I have sinned greatly," he sobbed. "Last night I slept with a woman and abandoned my vows. I am not worthy to enter the abbey at your side."

The teacher put his arm around the student and said, "We will enter the abbey together. And we will enter the cathedral together. And together we will confess your sin. No one but God will know which of the two of us fell."[1]

Doesn't that describe what God has done for us? When we kept our sin silent, we withdrew from him. We saw him as an enemy. We took steps to avoid his presence. But our confession of faults alters our perception. God is no longer a foe but a friend. We are at peace with him. He did more than the monk did, much more. More than share in our sin, Jesus was "crushed for the evil we did. The punishment, which made us well, was given to him" (Isa. 53:5). "He accepted the shame" (Heb. 12:2). He leads us into the presence of God.

Blessing #2: We Have a Place with God

Being ushered into God's presence is the second blessing Paul describes: "This happened through our Lord Jesus Christ, who has brought us into that blessing of God's grace that we now enjoy" (v. 2). Look at the phrase, "who has brought us into." The Greek word means "to usher into the presence of royalty." Twice in Ephesians Paul reminds us of our right to enter God's presence:

It is through Christ that all of us are able to come into the presence of the Father. (Eph. 2:18 TEV)

Now we can come fearlessly right into God's presence. . . . (Eph. 3:12 TLV)

Christ meets you outside the throne room, takes you by the hand, and walks you into the presence of God. Upon entrance we find grace, not condemnation; mercy, not punishment. Where we would never be granted an audience with the king, we are now welcomed into his presence.

If you are a parent you understand this. If a child you don't know appears on your doorstep and asks to spend the night, what would you do? Likely you would ask him his name, where he lives, find out why he is roaming the streets, and contact his parents. On the other hand, if a youngster enters your house escorted by your child, that child is welcome. The same is true with God. By becoming friends with the Son we gain access to the Father.

Jesus promised, "All who stand before others and say they believe in me, I will say before my Father in heaven that they belong to me" (Matt. 10:32). Because we are friends of his Son, we have entrance to the throne room. He ushers us into that "blessing of God's grace that we now enjoy" (Rom. 5:2).

This gift is not an occasional visit before God but rather a permanent "access by faith into this grace by which we now stand" (v. 2 NIV). Here is where my analogy with the replacement baseball players ceases. They knew their status was temporary. Their privilege lasted only as long as the strike continued. Not so with us.

Our privilege lasts as long as God is faithful, and his faithfulness has never been questioned. "If we are not faithful, he will still be faithful, because he cannot be false to himself" (2 Tim. 2:13). Isaiah described God's faithfulness as the "belt around his waist" (Isa. 11:5). David announces that the Lord's faithfulness "reaches to the heavens" (Ps. 36:5).

I suppose the baseball analogy would work if the team owner conferred upon us the status of lifetime team members. Upon doing so our position on the squad would not depend upon our performance but upon his power. Has an owner ever given such a gift? I don't know, but God has and God does.

Before moving on, note the sequence of these blessings. The first blessing deals with our past; we have peace with God because our past is pardoned. The second blessing deals with the present. We have a place with God because Jesus has presented us to his Father. Any guess what the next blessing will cover?

Blessing #3: We Share in His Glory

You got it: our future. "And we are happy because of the hope we have of sharing God's glory" (Rom. 5:2).

Because of God's grace we go from being people whose "throats are like open graves" (Ps. 5:9) to being participants of God's glory. We were washed up and put out; now we are called up and put in.

What does it mean to share in God's glory? May I devote a chapter to that question? (Why am I asking you? The book's already written.) Come with me from the world of baseball and replacement players to a scene of a king and a cripple. You'll understand what I mean in a few pages.

The Privilege of Paupers

But God shows his great love for us in this way: Christ died for us while we were still sinners. ROMANS 5:8

Warning: The content of this chapter is likely to cause hunger. You might want to read it in the kitchen.

My first ministry position was in Miami, Florida. In our congregation we had more than our share of southern ladies who loved to cook. I fit in well because I was a single guy who loved to eat. The church was fond of having Sunday evening potluck dinners, and about once a quarter they *feasted*.

Some church dinners live up to the "potluck" name. The cooks empty the pot, and you try your luck. Not so with this church. Our potlucks were major events. Area grocery stores asked us to advise them in advance so they could stock their shelves. Cookbook sales went up. People never before seen in the pews could be found in the food line. For the women it was an unofficial cookoff, and for the men it was an unabashed pigout.

My, it was good, a veritable cornucopia of Corningware. Juicy ham bathed in pineapple, baked beans, pickled relish, pecan pie . . . (Oops, I just drooled on my computer keyboard.) Ever wondered why there are so many hefty preachers? You enter the ministry for meals like those.

As a bachelor I counted on potluck dinners for my survival strategy. While others were planning what to cook, I was studying the storage techniques of camels. Knowing I should bring something, I'd make it a point to raid my kitchen shelves on Sunday afternoon. The result was pitiful: One time I took a half-empty jar of Planters peanuts; another time I made a half-dozen jelly sandwiches. One of my better offerings was an unopened sack of chips; a more meager gift was a can of tomato soup, also unopened.

Wasn't much, but no one ever complained. In fact, the way those ladies acted, you would've thought I brought the Thanksgiving turkey. They'd take my jar of peanuts and set it on the long table with the rest of the food and hand me a plate. "Go ahead, Max, don't be bashful. Fill up your plate." And I would! Mashed potatoes and gravy. Roast beef. Fried chicken. I took a little bit of everything, except the peanuts.

I came like a pauper and ate like a king!

Though Paul never attended a potluck, he would have loved the symbolism. He would say that Christ does for us precisely what those women did for me. He welcomes us to his table by virtue of his love and our request. It is not our offerings that grant us a place at the feast; indeed, anything we bring appears puny at his table.

Our admission of hunger is the only demand, for "Blessed are those who hunger and thirst for righteousness, for they shall be filled" (Matt. 5:6 NKJV).

Our hunger, then, is not a yearning to be avoided but rather a God-given desire to be heeded. Our weakness is not to be dismissed but to be confessed. Isn't this at the heart of Paul's words when he writes, "When we were unable to help ourselves, at the moment of our need, Christ died for us, although we were living against God. Very few people will die to save the life of someone else. Although perhaps for a good person someone might possibly die. But God shows his great love for us in this way: Christ died for us while we were still sinners" (Rom. 5:6–8).

The Portrait of a Pauper

Paul's portrait of us is not attractive. We were "unable to help ourselves," "living against God," "sinners," and "God's enemies" (Rom. 5:6, 8, 10). Such are the people for whom God died.

Family therapist Paul Faulkner tells of the man who set out to adopt a troubled teenage girl. One would question the father's logic. The girl was destructive, disobedient, and dishonest. One day she came home from school and ransacked the house looking for money. By the time he arrived, she was gone and the house was in shambles.

Upon hearing of her actions, friends urged him not to finalize the adoption. "Let her go," they said. "After all, she's not really your daughter." His response was simply. "Yes, I know. But I told her she was."[1]

God, too, has made a covenant to adopt his people. His covenant is not invalidated by our rebellion. It's one thing to love us when we are strong, obedient, and willing. But when we ransack his house and steal what is his? This is the test of love.

And God passes the test. "God shows his great love for us in this way: Christ died for us while we were still sinners" (5:8).

The ladies at our church didn't see me and my peanuts and say, "Come back when you've learned to cook."

The father didn't look at the wrecked house and say, "Come back when you've learned respect."

God didn't look at our frazzled lives and say, "I'll die for you when you deserve it."

Nor did David look at Mephibosheth and say, "I'll rescue you when you've learned to walk."

Mephibo-*what?*

Mephibosheth. When you hear his story you'll see why I mention his name. Blow the dust off the books of 1 and 2 Samuel, and there you'll see him.

> (Saul's son Jonathan had a son named Mephibosheth, who was crippled in both feet. He was five years old when the news came from Jezreel that Saul and Jonathan were dead. Mephibosheth's nurse had picked him up and run away. But as she hurried to leave, she dropped him, and now he was lame.) (2 Sam. 4:4)

The parentheses around the verse are not typos. Mephibosheth is bracketed into the Bible. The verse doesn't tell us much, just his name (Mephibosheth), his calamity (dropped by his nurse), his deformity (crippled), and then it moves on.

But that's enough to raise a few questions. Who was this boy? Why is this story in Scripture? Why is Lucado mentioning him in a book about grace? A bit of background would be helpful.

Mephibosheth was the son of Jonathan, the grandson of Saul, who was the first king of Israel. Saul and Jonathan were killed in battle, leaving the throne to be occupied by David. In those days the new king often staked out his territory by exterminating the family of the previous king.

David had no intention of following this tradition, but the family of Saul didn't know that. So they hurried to escape. Of special concern to them was five-year-old Mephibosheth, for upon the deaths of his father and uncle, he was the presumptive heir to the throne. If David was intent on murdering Saul's heirs, this boy would be first on his list. So the family got out of Dodge. But in the haste of the moment, Mephibosheth slipped from the arms of his nurse, permanently damaging both feet. For the rest of his life he would be a cripple.

If his story is beginning to sound familiar, it should. You and he have a lot in common. Weren't you also born of royalty? And don't you carry the wounds of a fall? And hasn't each of us lived in fear of a king we have never seen?

Mephibosheth would understand Paul's portrait of us paupers, "when we were unable to help ourselves . . ." (Rom. 5:6). For nearly two decades the young prince lived in a distant land, unable to walk to the king, too fearful to talk to the king. He was unable to help himself.

Meanwhile, David's kingdom flourished. Under his leadership, Israel grew to ten times its original size. He knew no defeat on the battlefield nor insurrection in his court. Israel was at peace. The people were thankful. And David, the shepherd made king, did not forget his promise to Jonathan.

The Promise of a King

David and Jonathan were like two keys on a piano keyboard. Alone they made music, but together they made harmony. Jonathan "loved David as much as he loved himself" (1 Sam. 20:17). Their legendary friendship met its ultimate test the day David learned that Saul was trying to kill him. Jonathan pledged to save David and asked his friend one favor in return: "You must never stop showing your kindness to my family, even when the LORD has destroyed all your enemies from the earth. So Jonathan made an agreement with David" (1 Sam. 20:15–16).

Don't you know this was a tender memory for David? Can't you imagine him reflecting on this moment years later? Standing on the balcony overlooking the safe city. Astride his steed riding through the abundant fields. Dressed in armor inspecting his capable army. Were there times when he was overwhelmed with gratitude? Were there times when he thought, *Had it not been for Jonathan saving my life, none of this would have happened?*

Perhaps such a moment of reflection prompted him to turn to his servants and ask, "Is anyone still left in Saul's family? I want to show kindness to that person for Jonathan's sake!" (2 Sam. 9:1).

Those in the grip of grace are known to ask such questions. Can't I do something for somebody? Can't I be kind to someone because others have been kind to me? This isn't a political maneuver. David isn't seeking to do good to be applauded by people. Nor is he doing something good so someone will do something for him. He is driven by the singular thought that he, too, was once weak. And in his weakness he was helped. David, while hiding from Saul, qualified for Paul's epitaph, "when we were unable to help ourselves" (Rom. 5:6).

David was delivered; now he desires to do the same. A servant named Ziba knows of a descendant. "'Jonathan has a son still living who is crippled in both feet.' The king asked Ziba, 'Where is this son?' Ziba answered, 'He is at the house of Makir son of Ammiel in Lo Debar'" (2 Sam. 9:3–4).

Just one sentence and David knew he had more than he bargained for. The boy was "crippled in both feet." Who would have blamed David for asking Ziba, "Are there any other options? Any healthy family members?"

Who would have faulted him for reasoning, *A cripple would not fit well into the castle crowd. Only the elite walk these floors; this kid can't even walk! And what service could he provide? No wealth, no education, no training. And who knows what he looks like? All these years he's been living in . . . what was it again? Lo Debar? Even the name means "barren place." Surely there is someone I can help who isn't so needy.*

But such words were never spoken. David's only response was, "Where is this son?" (v. 4).

This son. One wonders how long it had been since Mephibosheth was referred to as a son. In all previous references he was called a cripple. Every mention of him thus far is followed by his handicap. But the words of David make no mention of his affliction. He doesn't ask, "Where is Mephibosheth, this problem child?" but rather asks, "Where is this son?"

Many of you know what it's like to carry a stigma. Each time your name is mentioned, your calamity follows.

"Have you heard from John lately? You know, the fellow who got divorced?"

"We got a letter from Jerry. Remember him, the alcoholic?"

"Sharon is in town. What a shame that she has to raise those kids alone."

"I saw Melissa today. I don't know why she can't keep a job."

Like a pesky sibling, your past follows you wherever you go. Isn't there anyone who sees you for who you are and not what you did? Yes. There is One who does. Your King. When God speaks of you, he doesn't mention your plight, pain, or problem; he lets you share his glory. He calls you his child.

> He will not always accuse us,
> and he will not be angry forever.
> He has not punished us as our sins should be punished;
> he has not repaid us for the evil we have done.
> As high as the sky is above the earth,

so great is his love for those who respect him.
He has taken our sins away from us
    as far as the east is from the west.
The LORD has mercy on those who respect him,
    as a father has mercy on his children.
He knows how we were made;
    he remembers that we are dust. (Ps. 103:9–14)

Mephibosheth carried his stigma for twenty years. When people mentioned his name, they mentioned his problem. But when the king mentioned his name, he called him "son." And one word from the palace offsets a thousand voices in the streets.

David's couriers journeyed to Mephibosheth's door, carried him to a chariot, and escorted him to the palace. He was taken before the king, where he bowed facedown on the floor and confessed, "I am your servant" (2 Sam. 9:6). His fear is understandable. Though he may have been told that David was kind, what assurance did he have? Though the emissaries surely told him that David meant no harm, he was afraid. (Wouldn't you be?) The anxiety was on the face that faced the floor. David's first words to him were, "Don't be afraid."

By the way, your king has been known to say the same. Are you aware that the most repeated command from the lips of Jesus was, "Fear not"? Are you aware that the command from heaven not to be afraid appears in every book of the Bible?

Mephibosheth had been called, found, and rescued, but he still needed assurance. Don't we all? Don't we, like the trembling guest, need assurance that we are bowing before a gracious king? Paul says we have that assurance. The apostle points to the cross as our guarantee of God's love. "God shows his great love for us in this way: Christ died for us while we were still sinners" (Rom. 5:8). God proved his love for us by sacrificing his Son.

Formerly God had sent prophets to preach: Now he has sent his son to die. Earlier God commissioned angels to aid, now he has offered his son to redeem. When we tremble he points us to the splattered blood on the splintered beams and says, "Don't be afraid."

During the early days of the Civil War a Union soldier was arrested on charges of desertion. Unable to prove his innocence, he was condemned and sentenced to die a deserter's death. His appeal found its way to the desk of Abraham Lincoln. The president felt mercy for the soldier and signed a pardon. The soldier returned to service, fought the entirety of the war, and was killed in the last battle. Found within his breast pocket was the signed letter of the president.[2]

Close to the heart of the soldier were his leader's words of pardon. He found courage in grace. I wonder how many thousands more have found courage in the emblazoned cross of their king.

The Privilege of Adoption

Just as David kept his promise to Jonathan, so God keeps his promise to us. The name Mephibosheth means "he who scatters shame." And that is exactly what David intended to do for the young prince.

In swift succession David returned to Mephibosheth all his land, crops, and servants and then insisted that the cripple eat at the king's table. Not just once but four times!

"I will give you back all the land of your grandfather Saul, and *you will always eat at my table.*"

"Mephibosheth . . . *will always eat at my table.*"

"So *Mephibosheth ate at David's table* as if he were one of the king's sons."

"Mephibosheth lived in Jerusalem, because *he always ate at the king's table. And he was crippled in both feet.*" (2 Sam. 9:7, 10, 11, 13 *italics mine*)

Pause and envision the scene in the royal dining room. May I
turn my pen over to Charles Swindoll to assist you?

> The dinner bell rings through the king's palace and David comes to
> the head of the table and sits down. In a few moments Amnon—clever,
> crafty, Amnon—sits to the left of David. Lovely and gracious Tamar, a
> charming and beautiful young woman, arrives and sits beside Amnon.
> And then across the way, Solomon walks slowly from his study; preco-
> cious, brilliant, preoccupied Solomon. The heir apparent slowly sits
> down. And then Absalom—handsome, winsome Absalom with beau-
> tiful flowing hair, black as a raven, down to his shoulders—sits down.
> That particular evening Joab, the courageous warrior and David's com-
> mander of the troops, has been invited to dinner. Muscular, bronzed
> Joab is seated near the king. Afterward they wait. They hear the shuf-
> fling of feet, the clump, clump, clump of the crutches as Mephibosheth
> rather awkwardly finds his place at the table and slips into his seat . . .
> and the tablecloth covers his feet. I ask you: Did Mephibosheth under-
> stand grace?[3]

And I ask you, do you see our story in his?

Children of royalty, crippled by the fall, permanently marred by
sin. Living parenthetical lives in the chronicles of earth only to be
remembered by the king. Driven not by our beauty but by his
promise, he calls us to himself and invites us to take a permanent
place at his table. Though we often limp more than we walk, we
take our place next to the other sinners-made-saints and we share
in God's glory.

May I share a partial list of what awaits you at his table?

You are beyond condemnation (Rom. 8:1).

You are delivered from the law (Rom. 7:6).

You are near God (Eph. 2:13).

You are delivered from the power of evil (Col. 1:13).

You are a member of his kingdom (Col. 1:13).

You are justified (Rom. 5:1).

You are perfect (Heb. 10:14).

You have been adopted (Rom. 8:15).

You have access to God at any moment (Eph. 2:18).

You are a part of his priesthood (1 Pet. 2:5).

You will never be abandoned (Heb. 13:5).

You have an imperishable inheritance (1 Pet. 1:4).

You are a partner with Christ in life (Col. 3:4) and privilege (Eph. 2:6), suffering (2 Tim. 2:12), and service (1 Cor. 1:9).

You are a:

> member of his body (1 Cor. 12:13),
>
> branch in the vine (John 15:5),
>
> stone in the building (Eph 2:19–22),
>
> bride for the groom (Eph. 5:25–27),
>
> priest in the new generation (1 Pet. 2:9), and a
>
> dwelling place of the Spirit (1 Cor. 6:19).

You possess (get this!) every spiritual blessing possible. "In Christ, God has given us every spiritual blessing in the heavenly world" (Eph. 1:3). This is the gift offered to the lowliest sinner on earth. Who could make such an offer but God? "From him we all received one gift after another" (John 1:16).

Paul speaks for us all when he asks,

> Have you ever come on anything quite like this extravagant love of God, this deep, deep, wisdom? It's way over our heads. We'll never figure it out.

"Is there anyone around who can explain God?
Anyone smart enough to tell him what to do?

Anyone who has done him such a huge favor
    that God has to ask his advice?"
Everything comes from him;
Everything comes through him;
Everything ends up in him.
Always glory! Always praise!
        Yes. Yes. Yes. (Rom. 11:33–36 MSG)

Like Mephibosheth, we are sons of the King. And like me in
Miami, our greatest offering is peanuts compared to what we are
given.

PART THREE

WHAT A DIFFERENCE!

Where the grace of God is missed, bitterness is born.

But where the grace of God is embraced, forgiveness

flourishes.

The longer we walk in the garden,

the more likely we are to smell like flowers.

The more we immerse ourselves in grace, the more

likely we are to give grace.

11 | Grace Works

How can we who died to sin still live in it? ROMANS 6:2 RSV

Sometimes I give away money at the end of a sermon. Not to pay the listeners (though some may feel they've earned it) but to make a point. I offer a dollar to anyone who will accept it. Free money. A gift. I invite anyone who wants the cash to come and take it.

The response is predictable. A pause. Some shuffling of feet. A wife elbows her husband, and he shakes his head. A teen starts to stand and then remembers her reputation. A five-year-old starts walking down the aisle, and his mother pulls him back. Finally some courageous (or impoverished) soul stands up and says, "I'll take it!" The dollar is given, and the application begins.

"Why didn't you take my offer?" I ask the

rest. Some say they were too embarrassed. The pain wasn't worth the gain. Others feared a catch, a trick. And then there are those whose wallets are fat. What's a buck to someone who has hundreds?

Then the obvious follow-up question. "Why don't people accept Christ's free gift?" The answers are similar. Some are too embarrassed. To accept forgiveness is to admit sin, a step we are slow to take. Others fear a trick, a catch. Surely there is some fine print in the Bible. Others think, *Who needs forgiveness when you're as good as I am?*

The point makes itself. Though grace is available to all, it's accepted by few. Many choose to sit and wait while only a few choose to stand and trust.

Usually that is the end of it. The lesson is over, I'm a dollar poorer, one person is a dollar richer, and all of us are a bit wiser. Something happened a couple of weeks back, however, that added a new dimension to the exercise. Myrtle was the one who said yes to the dollar. I'd made the offer and was waiting for a taker when she yelled, "I'll take it!" Up she popped and down she came and I gave her the dollar. She took her seat, I made my point, and we all went home.

I ran into her a few days later and kidded her about making money off my sermons. "Do you still have the dollar?" I asked.

"No."

"Did you spend it?"

"No, I gave it away," she answered. "When I returned to my seat a youngster asked me if he could have it, and I said, 'Sure, it was a gift to me; it's a gift to you.'"

My, isn't that something? As simply as she received, she gave. As easily as it came, it went. The boy didn't beg, and she didn't struggle. How could she, who had been given a gift, not give a gift in return? She was caught in the grip of grace.

We'll use these final chapters to discuss the impact of grace. Now that we've considered the mess we made and the God we have, let's ponder what a difference grace makes in our lives. Exactly what does a grace-driven Christian look like?

Grace Releases Us

In Romans 6 Paul asks a crucial question: "How can we who died to sin still live in it?" (v. 2 RSV). How can we who have been made right not live righteous lives? How can we who have been loved not love? How can we who have been blessed not bless? How can we who have been given grace not live graciously?

Paul seems stunned that an alternative would even exist! How could grace result in anything but gracious living? "So do you think we should continue sinning so that God will give us even more grace? No!" (v. 1).

The two-dollar term for this philosophy is antinomianism: *anti*, meaning "against" and *nomos* meaning "moral law." Promoters of the idea see grace as a reason to do bad rather than a reason to do good. Grace grants them a ticket for evil. The worse I act the better God seems. This isn't Paul's first reference to the teaching. Remember Romans 3:7? "A person might say, 'When I lie, it really gives him the glory, because my lie shows God's truth.'"

What a scam. You mothers wouldn't tolerate it. Can you imagine your teenager saying, "Mom, I'll keep my room messy so the whole neighborhood can see what a good housekeeper you are"? A boss wouldn't let the employee say, "The reason I'm lazy is to give you an opportunity to display your forgiveness." No one respects the beggar who refuses to work, saying, "I'm just giving the government an opportunity to demonstrate benevolence."

We'd scoff at such hypocrisy. We wouldn't tolerate it, and we wouldn't do it.

Or would we? Let's answer that one slowly. Perhaps we don't sin *so* God can give grace, but do we ever sin *knowing* God will give grace? Do we ever compromise tonight, knowing we'll confess tomorrow?

It's easy to be like the fellow visiting Las Vegas who called the preacher, wanting to know the hours of the Sunday service. The preacher was impressed. "Most people who come to Las Vegas don't do so to go to church."

"Oh, I'm not coming for the church. I'm coming for the gambling and parties and wild women. If I have half as much fun as I intend to, I'll need a church come Sunday morning."

Is that the intent of grace? Is God's goal to promote disobedience? Hardly. "Grace . . . teaches us not to live against God nor to do the evil things the world wants us to do. Instead, that grace teaches us to live now in a wise and right way and in a way that shows we serve God" (Titus 2:11–12). God's grace has released us from selfishness. Why return?

The Penalty Has Been Paid

Think of it this way. Sin put you in prison. Sin locked you behind the bars of guilt and shame and deception and fear. Sin did nothing but shackle you to the wall of misery. Then Jesus came and paid your bail. He served your time; he satisfied the penalty and set you free. Christ died, and when you cast your lot with him, your old self died too.

The only way to be set free from the prison of sin is to serve its penalty. In this case the penalty is death. Someone has to die, either you or a heaven-sent substitute. You cannot leave prison unless there is a death. But that death has occurred at Calvary. And when Jesus died, you died to sin's claim on your life. You are free.

Near the city of Sao José dos Campos, Brazil, is a remarkable facility. Twenty years ago the Brazilian government turned a prison over to two Christians. The institution was renamed Humaita, and the plan was to run it on Christian principles. With the exception of two full-time staff, all the work is done by inmates. Families outside the prison adopt an inmate to work with during and after his term. Chuck Colson visited the prison and made this report:

When I visited Humaita I found the inmates smiling—particularly the murderer who held the keys, opened the gates and let me in. Wherever I walked I saw men at peace. I saw clean living areas, people working industriously. The walls were decorated with Biblical sayings from Psalms and Proverbs. . . . My guide escorted me to the notorious prison cell once used for torture. Today, he told me, that block houses only a single inmate. As we reached the end of a long concrete corridor and he put the key in the lock, he paused and asked, "Are you sure you want to go in?"

"Of course," I replied impatiently, "I've been in isolation cells all over the world." Slowly he swung open the massive door, and I saw the prisoner in that punishment cell: a crucifix, beautifully carved by the Humaita inmates—the prisoner Jesus, hanging on a cross.

"He's doing time for the rest of us," my guide said softly.[1]

Christ has taken your place. There is no need for you to remain in the cell. Ever heard of a discharged prisoner who wanted to stay? Nor have I. When the doors open, prisoners leave. The thought of a person preferring jail over freedom doesn't compute. Once the penalty is paid, why live under bondage? You are discharged from the penitentiary of sin. Why, in heaven's name, would you ever want to set foot in that prison again?

Paul reminds us: "Our old life died with Christ on the cross so that our sinful selves would have no power over us and we would not be slaves to sin. Anyone who has died is made free from sin's control" (Rom. 6:6–7).

He is not saying that it is impossible for believers to sin; he's say-

ing it is stupid for believers to sin. "It's not the literal impossibility .
. . . but the moral incongruity" of the saved returning to sin.[2]

What does the prison have that you desire? Do you miss the
guilt? Are you homesick for dishonesty? Do you have fond memo-
ries of being lied to and forgotten? Was life better when you were
dejected and rejected? Do you have a longing to once again see a
sinner in the mirror?

It makes no sense to go back to prison.

The Vow Has Been Made

Not only has a price been paid, a vow has been made. "Did you forget that all of us became part of Christ when we were baptized?"
(Rom. 6:2).

Baptism was no casual custom, no ho-hum ritual. Baptism was,
and is, "a pledge made to God from a good conscience" (1 Pet. 3:21
TJB).

Paul's high regard for baptism is demonstrated in the fact that he
knows all of his readers have been instructed in its importance.
"*You have been taught* that when we were baptized into Christ we
were baptized into his death" (Rom. 6:2 TJB, italics mine).

What form of amnesia is this? Like a bride horrified to see her
new husband flirting with women at the wedding reception, Paul
asks, "Did you forget your vows?"

Indeed, baptism is a vow, a sacred vow of the believer to follow
Christ. Just as a wedding celebrates the fusion of two hearts, baptism celebrates the union of sinner with Savior. We "became part
of Christ when we were baptized" (v. 2).

Do the bride and groom understand all of the implications of the
wedding? No. Do they know every challenge or threat they will

face? No. But they know they love each other and vow to be faithful to the end.

When a willing heart enters the waters of baptism, does he know the implications of the vow? No. Does she know every temptation or challenge? No. But both know the love of God and are responding to him.

Please understand, it is not the act that saves us. But it is the act that symbolizes how we are saved! The invisible work of the Holy Spirit is visibly dramatized in the water.

> That plunge beneath the running waters was like a death; the moment's pause while they swept overhead was like a burial; the standing erect once more in air and sunlight was a species of resurrection.[3]

Remove your shoes, bow your head, and bend your knees; this is a holy event. Baptism is not to be taken lightly.

To return to sin after sealing our souls in baptism is like committing, well, it's like committing adultery on your honeymoon. Can you imagine the distraught bride discovering her husband in the arms of another woman only days after hearing his vow at the altar? Among her many sizzling words will likely be the question, "Have you forgotten what you said to me?"

Similarly God asks, "Does our union mean nothing to you? Is our covenant so fragile that you would choose the arms of a harlot over mine?"

Who, in their right mind, would want to abandon these vows? Who will care for you more than Christ? Have we forgotten what life was like before our baptism? Have we forgotten the mess we were in before we were united with him? I choose the word *mess* intentionally. May I share a mess I'm glad I am out of? My bachelor's apartment.

Exposed to a Higher Standard

Of all the names I've been called, no one has ever accused me of being a neat freak. Some people have a high threshold of pain; I have a high threshold of sloppiness. Not that my mom didn't try. And not that she didn't succeed. As long as I was under her roof, I stacked my plate and picked up my shorts. But once I was free, I was free indeed.

Most of my life I've been a closet slob. I was slow to see the logic of neatness. Why make up a bed if you are going to sleep in it again tonight? Does it make sense to wash dishes after only one meal? Isn't it easier to leave your clothes on the floor at the foot of the bed so they'll be there when you get up and put them on? Is anything gained by putting the lid on the toothpaste tube tonight only to remove it again tomorrow?

I was as compulsive as anyone, only I was compulsive about being messy. Life was too short to match your socks; just buy longer pants!

Then I got married.

Denalyn was so patient. She said she didn't mind my habits . . . if I didn't mind sleeping outside. Since I did, I began to change.

I enrolled in a twelve-step program for slobs. ("My name is Max, I hate to vacuum.") A physical therapist helped me rediscover the muscles used for hanging shirts and placing toilet paper on the holder. My nose was reintroduced to the fragrance of Pine Sol. By the time Denalyn's parents came to visit, I was a new man. I could go three days without throwing a sock behind the couch.

But then came the moment of truth. Denalyn went out of town for a week. Initially I reverted to the old man. I figured I'd be a slob for six days and clean on the seventh. But something strange happened, a curious discomfort. I couldn't relax with dirty dishes in the sink. When I saw an empty potato-chip sack on the floor I—

hang on to your hat—bent over and picked it up! I actually put my bath towel back on the rack. What had happened to me?

Simple. I'd been exposed to a higher standard.

Isn't that what has happened with us? Isn't that the heart of Paul's argument? How could we who have been freed from sin return to it? Before Christ our lives were out of control, sloppy, and indulgent. We didn't even know we were slobs until we met him.

Then he moved in. Things began to change. What we threw around we began putting away. What we neglected we cleaned up. What had been clutter became order. Oh, there were and still are occasional lapses of thought and deed, but by and large he got our house in order.

Suddenly we find ourselves wanting to do good. Go back to the old mess? Are you kidding? "In the past you were slaves to sin—sin controlled you. But thank God, you fully obeyed the things that you were taught. You were made free from sin, and now you are slaves to goodness" (Rom. 6:17–18).

Can a discharged prisoner return to confinement? Yes. But let him remember the gray walls and the long nights. Can a newlywed forget his vows? Yes. But let him remember his holy vow and his beautiful bride. Can a converted slob once again be messy? Yes. But let him consider the difference between the filth of yesterday and the purity of today.

Can one who has been given a free gift not share that gift with others? I suppose. But let him remember Myrtle. Let him remember that he, like she, received a free gift. Let him remember that all of life is a gift of grace. And let him remember that the call of grace is to live a gracious life.

For that is how grace works.

Turning Yourself In

What a wretched man I am! ROMANS 7:24

Charles Robertson should have turned himself in. Not that he would've been acquitted; he robbed a bank. But at least he wouldn't have been the laughingstock of Virginia Beach.

Cash-strapped Robertson, nineteen, went to Jefferson State Bank on a Wednesday afternoon, filled out a loan application, and left. Apparently he changed his mind about the loan and opted for a quicker plan. He returned within a couple of hours with a pistol, a bag, and a note demanding money. The teller complied, and all of a sudden Robertson was holding a sack of loot.

Figuring the police were fast on their way, he dashed out the front door. He was halfway to the car when he realized he'd left the note. Fearing it could be used as evidence against him, he ran back into the bank and snatched it from the teller. Now holding the note and the money, he ran a block to his parked car. That's when he realized he'd left his keys on the counter when he'd returned for the note.

"At this point," one detective chuckled, "total panic set in."

Robertson ducked into the restroom of a fast-food restaurant. He dislodged a ceiling tile and hid the money and the .25 caliber hand-gun. Scampering through alleys and creeping behind cars, he finally reached his apartment where his roommate, who knew nothing of the robbery, greeted him with the words, "I need my car."

You see, Robertson's getaway vehicle was a loaner. Rather than confess to the crime and admit the bungle, Robertson shoveled yet another spade of dirt deeper into the hole. "Uh, uh, your car was stolen," he lied.

While Robertson watched in panic, the roommate called the police to inform them of the stolen vehicle. About twenty minutes later an officer spotted the "stolen" car a block from the recently robbed bank. Word was already on the police radio that the robber had forgotten his keys. The officer put two and two together and tried the keys on the car. They worked.

Detectives went to the address of the person who'd reported the missing car. There they found Robertson. He confessed, was charged with robbery, and put in jail. No bail. No loan. No kidding.

Some days it's hard to do anything right. It's even harder to do anything *wrong* right. Robertson's not alone. We've done the same. Perhaps we didn't take money but we've taken advantage or taken control or taken leave of our senses and then, like the thief, we've taken off. Dashing down alleys of deceit. Hiding behind buildings of work to be done or deadlines to be met. Though we try to act normal, anyone who looks closely at us can see we are on the lam:

Eyes darting and hands fidgeting, we chatter nervously. Committed to the cover-up, we scheme and squirm, changing the topic and changing direction. We don't want anyone to know the truth, especially God.

But from the beginning God has called for honesty. He's never demanded perfection, but he has expected truthfulness. As far back as the days of Moses, God said:

> If they will confess their sins and the sins of their fathers—their treachery against me and their hostility toward me, which made me hostile toward them so that I sent them into the land of their enemies—then . . . I will remember my covenant with Jacob and my covenant with Isaac and my covenant with Abraham, and I will remember the land. (Lev. 26:40–42 NIV)

Honest Hearts Lead to Honest Worship

Nehemiah knew the value of honesty. Upon hearing of the crumbled walls in Jerusalem, did he fault God? Did he blame heaven? Hardly. Read his prayer: "I confess the sins we Israelites have done against you. My father's family and I have sinned against you. We have been wicked toward you and have not obeyed the commands, rules, and laws you gave your servant Moses" (Neh. 1:6–7).

Here is the second most powerful man in the kingdom turning himself in, accepting responsibility for the downfall of his people. The scene of his personal confession, however, is nothing compared to the day the entire nation repented. "They stood and confessed their sins and their ancestors' sins. For a fourth of the day they stood where they were and read from the Book of Teachings of the Lord their God. For another fourth of the day they confessed their sins and worshiped the Lord their God" (Neh. 9:2–4).

Can you picture the event? Hundreds of people spending hours in prayer, not making requests but making confessions. "I'm guilty, God." "I've failed you, Father."

Such public honesty is common in Scripture. God instructed the high priest to "put both his hands on the head of the living goat, and he will confess over it all the sins and crimes of Israel. In this way Aaron will put the people's sins on the goat's head. . . . The goat will carry on itself all the people's sins to a lonely place in the desert. The man who leads the goat will let it loose there" (Lev. 16:21–22).

By virtue of this drama the people learned that God despises sin and God deals with sin. Before there could be honest worship, there had to be honest hearts.

The Motivation of Truth

Confession does for the soul what preparing the land does for the field. Before the farmer sows the seed he works the acreage, removing the rocks and pulling the stumps. He knows that seed grows better if the land is prepared. Confession is the act of inviting God to walk the acreage of our hearts. "There is a rock of greed over here Father, I can't budge it. And that tree of guilt near the fence? Its roots are long and deep. And may I show you some dry soil, too crusty for seed?" God's seed grows better if the soil of the heart is cleared.

And so the Father and the Son walk the field together; digging and pulling, preparing the heart for fruit. Confession invites the Father to work the soil of the soul.

Confession seeks pardon from God, not amnesty. Pardon presumes guilt; amnesty, derived from the same Greek word as *amnesia*, "forgets" the alleged offense without imputing guilt. Confession admits wrong and seeks forgiveness; amnesty denies wrong and claims innocence.

Many mouth a prayer for forgiveness while in reality claiming amnesty. Consequently our worship is cold (why thank God for a grace we don't need?) and our faith is weak (I'll handle my mistakes myself, thank you). We are better at keeping God out than we are at inviting God in. Sunday mornings are full of preparing the body for worship, preparing the hair for worship, preparing the clothes for worship . . . but preparing the soul?

Am I missing the mark when I say that many of us attend church on the run? Am I out of line when I say many of us *spend life on the run?*

Am I overstating the case when I announce, "Grace means you don't have to run anymore!"? It's the truth. Grace means it's finally safe to turn ourselves in.

A Model of Truth

Peter did. Remember Peter? "Flash the sword and deny the Lord" Peter? The apostle who boasted one minute and bolted the next? He snoozed when he should have prayed. He denied when he should have defended. He cursed when he should have comforted. He ran when he should have stayed. We remember Peter as the one who turned and fled, but do we remember Peter as the one who returned and confessed? We should.

I've got a question for you.

How did the New Testament writers know of his sin? Who told them of his betrayal? And, more importantly, how did they know the details? Who told them of the girl at the gate and the soldiers starting the fire? How did Matthew know it was Peter's accent that made him a suspect? How did Luke learn of the stare of Jesus? Who told all four of the crowing rooster and flowing tears?

The Holy Spirit? I suppose. Could be that each writer learned of the moment by divine inspiration. Or, more likely, each learned of the betrayal by an honest confession. Peter turned himself in. Like the bank robber, he bungled it and ran. Unlike the robber, Peter stopped and thought. Somewhere in the Jerusalem shadows he quit running, fell to his knees, buried his face in his hands, and gave up.

But not only did he give up, he opened up. He went back to the room where Jesus had broken the bread and shared the wine. (It says a lot about the disciples that they let Peter back in the door.)

There he is, every burly bit of him filling the doorframe. "Fellows, I've got something to get off my chest." And that's when they learn of the fire and the girl and the look from Jesus. That's when they hear of the cursing mouth and the crowing rooster. That's how they heard the story. He turned himself in.

How can I be so sure? Two reasons.

1. *He couldn't stay away.* When word came that the tomb was empty, who was first out of the room? Peter. When word came that Jesus was on the shore, who was first out of the boat? Peter. He was on the run again. Only now he was running in the right direction.

Here is a good rule of thumb: Those who keep secrets from God keep their distance from God. Those who are honest with God draw near to God.

This is nothing novel. It happens between people. If you loan me your car and I wreck it, will I look forward to seeing you again? No. It is no coincidence that the result of the very first sin was to duck into the bushes. Adam and Eve ate the fruit, heard God in the garden, and crept behind the leaves.

"Where are you?" God asked, not for his benefit. He knew exactly where they were. The question was spiritual, not geographical. "Examine where you are, children. You aren't where you were. You were at my side; now you have hidden from me."

Secrets erect a fence while confession builds a bridge.

Once there were a couple of farmers who couldn't get along with each other. A wide ravine separated their two farms, but as a sign of their mutual distaste for each other, each constructed a fence on his side of the chasm to keep the other out.

In time, however, the daughter of one met the son of the other, and the couple fell in love. Determined not to be kept apart by the folly of their fathers, they tore down the fence and used the wood to build a bridge across the ravine.

Confession does that. Confessed sin becomes the bridge over which we can walk back into the presence of God.

There is a second reason I'm confident of Peter's confession.

2. *He couldn't stay silent.* Only fifty days after denying Christ, Peter is preaching Christ. Peter cursed his Lord at the Passover. He proclaimed his Lord at the feast. This is not the action of a fugitive. What took him from traitor to orator? He let God deal with the secrets of his life. "Confess your sins to each other and pray for each other so that God can heal you" (James 5:16).

"If we confess our sins, he will forgive our sins, because we can trust God to do what is right. He will cleanse us from all the wrongs we have done" (1 John 1:9).

The fugitive lives in fear, but the penitent lives in peace.

The Moment of Truth

Again, Jesus has never demanded that we be perfect, only that we be honest. "You want me to be completely truthful" wrote David (Ps. 51:6). But honesty is a stubborn virtue for most. "Me, a thief?" we ask with revolver in one hand and bag of loot in the other.

It wasn't easy for Peter. He considered himself the MVA (most valuable apostle). Wasn't he one of the early draft picks? Wasn't he one of the chosen three? Didn't he confess Christ while the others were silent? Peter never thought he needed help until he lifted his eyes from the fire and saw the eyes of Jesus. "While Peter was still speaking a rooster crowed. Then the Lord turned and looked straight at Peter" (Luke 22:60–61).

Jesus and Peter are not the only two in the midnight street, but they might as well be. Jesus is surrounded by accusers, but he doesn't respond. He's encircled by enemies, but he doesn't react. The night air is full of taunts, but Jesus doesn't hear. But let one follower slip when he should have stood and the Master's head pops up and his eyes search through the shadows and the disciple knows.

"The Lord looks down from heaven and sees every person. From his throne he watches all who live on earth. He made their hearts and understands everything they do" (Ps. 33:13–15).

You know when God knows. You know when he is looking. Your heart tells you. Your Bible tells you. Your mirror tells you. The longer you run, the more complicated life gets. But the sooner you confess, the lighter your load becomes. David knew this. He wrote:

> When I kept things to myself,
> I felt weak deep inside me.
> I moaned all day long.
> Day and night you punished me.
> My strength was gone as in the summer heat.
> Then I confessed my sins to you
> and didn't hide my guilt.
> I said, "I will confess my sins to the LORD,"
> and you forgave my guilt. (Ps. 32:3–5)

These verses remind me of a mistake I made in high school. (My mother says I shouldn't use my juvenile foibles for illustrations. But I have so many!) Our baseball coach had a firm rule against chewing tobacco. We had a couple of players who were known to sneak a chew, and he wanted to call it to our attention.

He got our attention, all right. Before long we'd all tried it. A sure test of manhood was to take a chew when the pouch was passed down the bench. I had barely made the team; I sure wasn't going to fail the test of manhood.

One day I'd just popped a plug in my mouth when one of the players warned, "Here comes the coach!" Not wanting to get caught, I did what came naturally, I swallowed. *Gulp.*

I added new meaning to the scripture, "I felt weak deep inside me. I moaned all day long. . . . My strength was gone as in the summer heat." I paid the price for hiding my disobedience.

My body was not made to ingest tobacco. Your soul was not made to ingest sin.

May I ask a frank question? Are you keeping any secrets from God? Any parts of your life off limits? Any cellars boarded up or attics locked? Any part of your past or present that you hope you and God never discuss?

Learn a lesson from the robber: The longer you run, the worse it gets. Learn a lesson from Peter: The sooner you speak to Jesus, the more you'll speak for Jesus. And take a pointer from a nauseated third baseman. You'll feel better if you get it out.

Once you're in the grip of grace, you're free to be honest. Turn yourself in before things get worse. You'll be glad you did.

Honest to God, you will.

13 | Sufficient Grace

2 Corinthians
12:7–9

*To keep me from becoming conceited
because of these surpassingly great revela-
tions, there was given me a thorn in my
flesh, a messenger of Satan to torment me.
Three times I pleaded with the Lord to take
it away from me. But he said to me,
'My grace is sufficient for you, my power
is made perfect in weakness.'"*

2 CORINTHIANS 12:7–9 NIV

Here is the scene: You and I and a half-dozen
other folks are flying across the country in a
chartered plane. All of a sudden the engine
bursts into flames, and the pilot rushes out of
the cockpit.

"We're going to crash!" he yells. "We've
got to bail out!"

Good thing he knows where the parachutes are because we don't. He passes them
out, gives us a few pointers, and we stand in
line as he throws open the door. The first
passenger steps up to the door and shouts
over the wind, "Could I make a request?"

"Sure, what is it?"

"Any way I could get a pink parachute?"

The pilot shakes his head in disbelief. "Isn't it enough that I gave you a parachute at all?" And so the first passenger jumps.

The second steps to the door. "I'm wondering if there is any way you could ensure that I won't get nauseated during the fall?"

"No, but I can ensure that you will have a parachute for the fall."

Each of us comes with a request and receives a parachute.

"Please captain," says one, "I am afraid of heights. Would you remove my fear?"

"No," he replies, "but I'll give you a parachute."

Another pleads for a different strategy, "Couldn't you change the plans? Let's crash with the plane. We might survive."

The pilot smiles and says, "You don't know what you are asking" and gently shoves the fellow out the door. One passenger wants some goggles, another wants boots, another wants to wait until the plane is closer to the ground.

"You people don't understand," the pilot shouts as he "helps" us, one by one. "I've given you a parachute; that is enough."

Only one item is necessary for the jump, and he provides it. He places the strategic tool in our hands. The gift is adequate. But are we content? No. We are restless, anxious, even demanding.

Too crazy to be possible? Maybe in a plane with pilots and parachutes, but on earth with people and grace? God hears thousands of appeals per second. Some are legitimate. We, too, ask God to remove the fear or change the plans. He usually answers with a gentle shove that leaves us airborne and suspended by his grace.

The Problem: When God Says No

There are times when the one thing you want is the one thing you never get. You're not being picky or demanding; you're only obeying his command to "ask God for everything you need" (Phil. 4:6).

All you want is an open door or an extra day or an answered prayer, for which you will be thankful.

And so you pray and wait.

No answer.

You pray and wait.

No answer.

You pray and wait.

May I ask a very important question? What if God says no?

What if the request is delayed or even denied? When God says no to you, how will you respond? If God says, "I've given you my grace, and that is enough," will you be content?

Content. That's the word. A state of heart in which you would be at peace if God gave you nothing more than he already has. Test yourself with this question: What if God's only gift to you were his grace to save you. Would you be content? You beg him to save the life of your child. You plead with him to keep your business afloat. You implore him to remove the cancer from your body. What if his answer is, "My grace is enough." Would you be content?

You see, from heaven's perspective, grace *is* enough. If God did nothing more than save us from hell, could anyone complain? If God saved our souls and then left us to spend our lives leprosy-struck on a deserted island, would he be unjust? Having been given eternal life, dare we grumble at an aching body? Having been given heavenly riches, dare we bemoan earthly poverty?

Let me be quick to add, God has not left you with "just salvation." If you have eyes to read these words, hands to hold this book, the means to own this volume, he has already given you grace upon grace. The vast majority of us have been saved and then blessed even more!

But there are those times when God, having given us his grace, hears our appeals and says, "My grace is sufficient for you." Is he being unfair?

In *God Came Near* I've told how our oldest daughter fell into a swimming pool when she was two years old. A friend saw her and pulled her to safety.[1] What I didn't tell was what happened the next morning in my prayer time. I made a special effort to record my gratitude in my journal. I told God how wonderful he was for saving her. As clearly as if God himself were speaking, this question came to mind: *Would I be less wonderful had I let her drown? Would I be any less a good God for calling her home? Would I still be receiving your praise this morning had I not saved her?*

Is God still a good God when he says no?

The Plea: Remove the Thorn

Paul wrestled with that one. He knew the angst of unanswered prayer. At the top of his prayer list was an unidentified request that dominated his thoughts. He gave the appeal a code name: "a thorn in my flesh" (2 Cor. 12:7 NIV). Perhaps the pain was too intimate to put on paper. Maybe the request was made so often he reverted to shorthand. "I'm here to talk about the thorn again, Father." Or could it be that by leaving the appeal generic, Paul's prayer could be our prayer? For don't we all have a thorn in the flesh?

Somewhere on life's path our flesh is pierced by a person or a problem. Our stride becomes a limp, our pace is slowed to a halt, we try to walk again only to wince at each effort. Finally we plead with God for help.

Such was the case with Paul. (By the way, don't you find it encouraging that even Paul had a thorn in the flesh? There is comfort in learning that one of the writers of the Bible wasn't always on the same page with God.)

You don't get a thorn unless you're on the move, and Paul never stopped. Thessalonica, Jerusalem, Athens, Corinth—if he wasn't preaching he was in prison because of his preaching. But his walk was hampered by this thorn. The barb pierced through the sole of his sandal and into the soul of his heart and soon became a matter of intense prayer. "I begged the Lord three times to take this problem away from me" (2 Cor. 12:8).

This was no casual request, no P.S. in a letter. It was the first plea of the first sentence. "Dear God, I need some help!"

Nor was this a superficial prickle. It was a "stabbing pain" (PHILLIPS). Every step he took sent a shudder up his leg. Three different times he limped over to the side of the trail and prayed. His request was clear, and so was God's response, "My grace is sufficient" (v. 9 NIV).

What was this thorn in the flesh? No one knows for sure, but here are the top candidates.

1. *Sexual temptation.* Paul battling the flesh? Maybe. After all, Paul was a single man. He describes the temptress like one who knew her firsthand. "I want to do the things that are good, but I do not do them. I do not do the good things I want to do, but I do the bad things I do not want to do" (Rom. 7:18–19). Is Paul asking God to once and for all deliver him from the thirst for forbidden waters?

2. Perhaps the problem was not the flesh but *foes*; not temptation but opposition. The passage hints at this possibility. "This problem was a messenger from Satan," (2 Cor. 12:7). Paul had his share of opponents. There were those who questioned his apostleship (2 Cor. 12:12). There were some who undermined his message of grace (Gal. 1:7). By the way, when Paul wrote that this "messenger of Satan" was sent "to beat me," he wasn't exaggerating. Remove his robe and look at the scars. Or, since you can't do that, read of his attacks.

> I have been near death many times. Five times the Jews have given me their punishment of thirty-nine lashes with a whip. Three different times I was beaten with rods. One time I was almost stoned to death. Three times I was in ships that wrecked, and one of those times I spent

a night and a day in the sea. I have gone on many travels and have been in danger from rivers, thieves, my own people, the Jews, and those who are not Jews. I have been in danger in cities, in places where no one lives, and on the sea. And I have been in danger with false Christians. (2 Cor. 11:23–26)

Could anyone fault Paul for asking for a reprieve? A body can endure only so much. One grows weary living in the cross hairs of Satan's scope. "God, what if we limit this year to verbal attacks and let my sores heal? Or could we stagger the whippings and the stonings so they don't come at the same time? I've got a bruise on my neck that wakes me up each time I roll over. And remember the night in the jail in Philippi? My back hasn't recovered yet."

3. Of course, there were those who thought Paul deserved every lash, which leads us to a third option. Some think the thorn was his *abrasive nature*. Whatever he learned at the feet of Gamaliel, he may have dozed off the day they discussed the topic of tact. Before he knew grace, he had killed Christians. After he knew grace, he grilled the Christians. Example? "When Peter came to Antioch, I challenged him to his face, because he was wrong" (Gal. 2:11). Written like a true diplomat. In Paul's view you were on God's side or Satan's side, and should you slide from the first to the second he didn't keep it a secret, "Hymenaeus and Alexander have done that, and I have given them to Satan so they will learn not to speak against God" (1 Tim. 1:20).

Everyone within range of his tongue and pen knew how he felt and knew when to duck.

4. On the other hand, a case can be made that the thorn was not temptation, opposition, or public relation skills; it could have been *his body*. Remember his words at the end of one of his letters? "See what large letters I use to write this myself" (Gal. 6:11). Maybe his

eyes were bad. Could be he never got over that trip to Damascus. God got his attention with a light so bright Paul was left blind for three days. Maybe he never fully recovered. His clear vision of the cross may have come at the cost of a clear vision of anything else. He wrote of the Galatians that, "you would have taken out your eyes and given them to me if that were possible" (4:15).

In Paul's profession poor eyesight could be an occupational hazard. It's hard to travel if you can't see the trail. Not easy to write epistles if you can't see the page. Poor vision leads to strained eyes, which leads to headaches, which leads to long nights and long prayers for relief. "God, any chance I could see?"

It's hard to impress the crowd if you're making eye contact with a tree thinking it's a person. Which brings to mind one final possibility.

5. We assume Paul was a dynamic speaker, but those who heard him might disagree. "His speaking is nothing," he overheard them say in Corinth (2 Cor. 10:10). The apostle didn't argue with them. "When I came to you, I was weak and fearful and trembling. My teaching and preaching were not with words of wisdom that persuade people but proof of the power that the spirit gives" (1 Cor. 2:3–4). Translation? *I was so scared that I stuttered, so nervous that I forgot my point, and the fact that you heard anything at all is testimony to God.*

Let's back away for a minute and tally this up. (I don't know how you envisioned Paul, but that image may be about to change.) Tempted often. Beaten regularly. Opinionated. Dim-sighted. Thick-tongued. Is this the apostle Paul? (Could be he never got married because he couldn't get a date.) No wonder some questioned if he were an apostle.

And no wonder he prayed.

The Principle: Grace Is Enough

Are any of these requests inappropriate? Wouldn't he have been a better apostle with no temptation, no enemies, a calm demeanor, good eyes, and a glib tongue?

Maybe, but then again, maybe not.

Had God removed temptation, Paul may never have embraced God's grace. Only the hungry value a feast, and Paul was starving. The self-given title on his office door read, "Paul, Chief of Sinners." No pen ever articulated grace like Paul's. That may be because no person ever appreciated grace like Paul.

Had God stilled the whips, Paul may have never known love. "If I were burned alive for preaching the Gospel but didn't love others, it would be no value whatsoever" (1 Cor. 13:3 TLB). Persecution distills motives. In the end Paul's motives were distilled to one force, "the love of Christ controls us" (2 Cor. 5:14).

Had God made him meek and mild, who would have faced the legalists and confronted the hedonists and challenged the judgmentalists? The reason the letter of Galatians is in your Bible is because Paul couldn't stomach a diluted grace. Attribute the letters to Corinth to Paul's intolerance of sloppy faith. Paul's honesty may not have made many friends, but it sure made many disciples.

And Paul's eyes. If God had healed his eyesight, would Paul have had such insights? While the rest of the world was watching the world, Paul was seeing visions too great for words (2 Cor. 12:3–4).

And public speaking? Nothing intoxicates like the approval of the crowd. God may have just been keeping his apostle sober. Whatever the affliction, it was there for a purpose. And Paul knew it: "To keep me from becoming conceited." The God who despises pride did whatever necessary to keep Paul from becoming proud.

In this case, he simply told him, "My grace is sufficient." In your case, he may be saying the same thing.

You wonder why God doesn't remove temptation from your life? If he did, you might lean on your strength instead of his grace. A few stumbles might be what you need to convince you: His grace is sufficient for your sin.

You wonder why God doesn't remove the enemies in your life? Perhaps because he wants you to love like he loves. Anyone can love a friend, but only a few can love an enemy. So what if you aren't everyone's hero? His grace is sufficient for your self-image.

You wonder why God doesn't alter your personality? You, like Paul, are a bit rough around the edges? Say things you later regret or do things you later question? Why doesn't God make you more like him? He is. He's just not finished yet. Until he is, his grace is sufficient to overcome your flaws.

You wonder why God doesn't heal you? He *has* healed you. If you are in Christ, you have a perfected soul and a perfected body. His plan is to give you the soul now and the body when you get home. He may choose to heal parts of your body before heaven. But if he doesn't, don't you still have reason for gratitude? If he never gave you more than eternal life, could you ask for more than that? His grace is sufficient for gratitude.

Wonder why God won't give you a skill? If only God had made you a singer or a runner or a writer or a missionary. But there you are, tone-deaf, slow of foot and mind. Don't despair. God's grace is still sufficient to finish what he began. And until he's finished, let Paul remind you that the power is in the message, not the messenger. His grace is sufficient to speak clearly even when you don't.

For all we don't know about thorns, we can be sure of this. God would prefer we have an occasional limp than a perpetual strut. And if it takes a thorn for him to make his point, he loves us enough not to pluck it out.

God has every right to say no to us. We have every reason to say thanks to him. The parachute is strong, and the landing will be safe. His grace is sufficient.

The Civil War of the Soul

I was alive before I knew the law. But when the law's command came to me, then sin began to live and I died. The command was meant to bring life, but for me it brought death. . . . When I want to do good, evil is there with me. In my mind, I am happy with God's law. But I see another law working in my body, which makes war against the law that my mind accepts. That other law working in my body is the law of sin, and it makes me its prisoner. What a miserable man I am! Who will save me from this body that brings me death? ROMANS 7:9–10, 21–24

The following paragraphs document the degeneration of this author into criminal activity. The facts are true, and no names have been changed. I confess. I have violated the law. What's worse, I don't want to stop!

My felonious actions began innocently. My route to the office takes me south to an intersection where I and every other person in Texas turn east. Each morning I wait *long* minutes in a *long* line at a *long* light, always mumbling, "There must be a better way." A few days back I found it. While still a half-mile from the light, I spotted a shortcut, an alley behind a shopping center. It was worth a try. I turned on my blinker, made a quick left, bid farewell to the crawling commuters, and took my chances. I weaved in between the dumpsters and over the speed bumps and *voila*. It worked! The alley led me to my eastbound avenue several minutes faster than the rest of society.

Lewis and Clark would have been proud. I certainly was. From then on, I was ahead of the pack. Every morning while the rest of the cars waited in line, I veered onto my private autobahn and smugly applauded myself for seeing what others missed. I was surprised that no one had discovered it earlier, but then again, few have my innate navigational skills.

One morning Denalyn was with me in the car. "I'm about to remind you why you married me," I told her as we drew near to the intersection. "See that long line of cars? Hear that dirge from the suburbs? See that humdrum of humanity? It's not for me. Hang on!"

Like a hunter on a safari, I swerved from the six-lane onto the one-lane and shared with my sweetheart my secret expressway to freedom. "What do you think?" I asked her, awaiting her worship.

"I think you broke the law."

"What?"

"You just went the wrong way on a one-way street."

"I did not."

"Go back and see for yourself."

I did. She was right. Somehow I'd missed the sign. My road-less-taken was a route-not-permitted. Next to the big orange dumpster was a "Do Not Enter" sign. No wonder people gave me those looks when I turned into the alley. I thought they were envious; they thought I was deviant.

But my problem is not what I did before I knew the law. My

problem is what I want to do now, after I know the law. You'd think that I would have no desire to use the alley, but I do! Part of me still wants the shortcut. Part of me wants to break the law. (Forgive me all you patrolmen who are reading this book). Each morning the voices within me have this argument:

My "ought to" says, "It's illegal."

My "want to" answers, "But I've never been caught."

My "ought to" reminds, "The law is the law."

My "want to" counters, "But the law isn't for careful drivers like me. Besides, the five minutes I save I'll dedicate to prayer."

My "ought to" doesn't buy it. "Pray in the car."

Before I knew the law, I was at peace. Now that I know the law, an insurrection has occurred. I'm a torn man. On one hand I know what to do, but I don't want to do it. My eyes read the sign "Do Not Enter," but my body doesn't want to obey. What I should do and end up doing are two different matters. I was better off not knowing the law.

Sound familiar? It could. For many it is the itinerary of the soul. Before coming to Christ we all had our share of shortcuts. Immorality was a shortcut to pleasure. Cheating was a shortcut to success. Boasting was a shortcut to popularity. Lying was a shortcut to power.

Then we found Christ, we found grace, and we saw the signs. Hasn't it happened to you? You've got a hot temper and then read, "If you are angry with a brother or sister, you will be judged" (Matt. 5:22). *Wow, I never knew that.*

You've got wandering eyes and then read, "If anyone looks at a woman and wants to sin sexually with her, in his mind he has already done that sin with the woman" (Matt. 5:28). *Oh my, now what do I do?*

You tend to exaggerate to make your point and then discover, "Say only yes if you mean yes, and no if you mean no. If you say more than yes or no, it is from the Evil One" (Matt. 5:37). *But I've been talking like this for years.*

You enjoy letting people see your generosity and then read, "So when you give to the poor, don't let anyone know what you are doing" (Matt. 6:3). *Oh boy, I didn't know that was wrong.*

You have a habit of categorizing people into neat boxes and then hear Jesus say, "Don't judge other people, or you will be judged" (Matt. 7:1). *Son of a gun, no one ever told me judging was a sin.*

All these years you've been taking shortcuts, never seeing the "Do Not Enter" sign. But now you see it. Now you know it. I know, I know . . . it would have been easier had you never seen the sign, but now the law has been revealed. So what do you do?

Your battle is identical to the one within the heart of Paul.

> But I need something *more!* For if I know the law but still can't keep it, and if the power of sin within me keeps sabotaging my best intentions, I obviously need help! I realize that I don't have what it takes. I can will it, but I can't *do* it. I decide to do good, but I don't *really* do it; I decide not to do bad, but then I do it anyway. My decisions, such as they are, don't result in actions. Something has gone wrong deep within me and gets the better of me every time.
>
> It happens so regularly that it's predictable. The moment I decide to do good, sin is there to trip me up. I truly delight in God's commands, but it's pretty obvious that not all of me joins in that delight. Parts of me covertly rebel, and just when I least expect it, they take charge. (Rom. 7:14–23 MSG)

The civil war of the soul.

How *welcome* is Paul's confession! How good to know he struggled like the rest of us. Those who have been amazed by grace have been equally amazed by their sin. Why do I say yes to God one day and yes to Satan the next? Once I know God's commands, why am I not eager to obey them? Shouldn't these conflicts cease now that I see the sign? Does my struggle mean I'm not saved?

These are the questions of Romans 7. And these are the questions of many Christians. Some years ago I witnessed one man's inner war and chronicled these thoughts:

From where I sit I can see a redbird. He is on the roof across from my office. He has been there for three days. A splendid sight: deep crimson chest, crown of feathers which stands upon command. He sings the same song over and over—a long chirp followed by four short ones. The rhythm never varies. The pattern never changes.

He flies to the top of the building and perches on the highest point of the roof. He opens the feathered fan on the back of his neck, cocks his head back, and calls, "Chiiirrrup, chirp, chirp, chirp, chirp." Then he stands as if looking for the one he called to respond. But there is never an answer.

He will repeat the effort. The feathers will flash and the call will sound and he will wait. But there is never a reply.

After a few moments he will nosedive into the patio. He will see his reflection in a plate-glass window and fly into it—beak first. The crash will echo in the patio, and he will retreat. For just a moment. He gathers himself, then sees his reflection and off he goes . . . *slap!* Backward he staggers, scrambling to keep control, only to open his eyes and see the reflection and "*Pop!*" the sad drama is repeated.

I shake my head. "Why won't you learn?" I wonder. "How many times will it take for you to learn that the bird in the window is only an illusion?"

But he remains . . . flying into windows.

Minutes later a young man walks into my office. Sharp, well-dressed. Firm handshake, tanned face, flashy smile. Small talk about basketball, busy work schedules, and airports. I'm tempted to cut the chatter short . . . but don't. He needs time to gather courage. We know why he is here. We've had this talk before. He has a wife. He has a lover. He abandoned the first and lives with the second.

"Have you gone home?" I ask.

"No," he sighs, looking through the window into the patio. "I tried, but I didn't."

"Have you spoken to your wife?"

"I haven't got the nerve."

"He's just a kid," I say to myself. Underneath the Italian suit and sharp talk, he's a frightened six-year-old who knows he shouldn't but doesn't know how to stop. What is this vacuum within him that can't be filled by marriage? What is this passion which takes him to other beds?

I look out the window over his shoulder and see the redbird slap his beak against the pane. I look across my desk and see the man bury his face in his hands. "I know what I should do, but I can't."

What will it take for both to stop? How long will they hurt themselves before they wake up?

The next day I came to the office and the bird was gone. Soon after I called the man and he was gone. I think the bird learned a lesson. I'm not sure the man ever did.

Maybe you've hit your head against the wall. Are there weaknesses within you that stun you? Your words? Your thoughts? Your temper? Your greed? Your grudge? Your gossip? Things were better before you knew the law existed. But now you know. And now you have a war to wage. And I have two truths about grace for you to take into battle.

1. He Still Claims You

First of all, remember your position—you are a child of God. Some interpret the presence of the battle as the abandonment of God. Their logic goes something like this: "I am a Christian. My desires, however, are anything but Christian. No child of God would have these battles. I must be an orphan. God may have given me a place back then, but he has no place for me now."

That's Satan sowing those seeds of shame. If he can't seduce you with your sin, he'll let you sink in your guilt. Nothing pleases him more than for you to cower in the corner, embarrassed that you're still dealing with some old habit. "God's tired of your struggles," he whispers. "Your father is weary of your petitions for forgiveness," he lies.

And many believe him, spending years convinced that they are disqualified from the kingdom. *Can I go to the well of grace too many times? I don't deserve to ask for forgiveness again.*

Forgive my abrupt response, but who told you that you deserved forgiveness the first time? When you came to Christ did he know every sin you'd committed up until that point? Yes. Did Christ know every sin you would commit in the future? Yes, he knew that too. So Jesus saved you, knowing all the sins you would ever commit until the end of your life? Yes. You mean he is willing to call you his child even though he knows each and every mistake of your past and future? Yes.

Sounds to me like God has already proven his point. If your sin were too great for his grace, he never would have saved you in the first place. Your temptation isn't late-breaking news in heaven. Your sin doesn't surprise God. He saw it coming. Is there any reason to think that the One who received you the first time won't receive you every time?

Besides, the very fact that you are under attack must mean that you're on the right side. Did you notice who else had times of struggle? Paul did. Note the tense in which Paul is writing:

I *do* not understand . . ."

". . . it *is* sin living in me . . ."

"I *do* not *do* the good things I *want* . . ."

"I *see* another law working in my body . . ."

"What a miserable man I *am*" (see Rom. 7:14–25, italics mine).

Paul is writing in the present tense. He is not describing a struggle of the past; but a struggle in the present. For all we know, Paul was engaged in spiritual combat even as he wrote this letter. *You mean the apostle Paul battled sin while he was writing a book in the Bible?* Can you think of a more strategic time for Satan to attack?

Is it possible that Satan feared the fruit of this epistle to the Romans?

Could it be that he fears the fruits of your life? Could it be that you are under attack—not because you are so weak but because you might become so strong? Perhaps he hopes that in defeating you today he will have one less missionary or writer or giver or singer to fight with tomorrow.

2. He Still Guides You

Let me give you a second truth to take to the battlefield. The first was your position: You are a child of God. The second is your principle: the Word of God.

When under attack, our tendency is to question the validity of God's commands; we rationalize like I do with the one-way street. *The law is for others, not for me. I'm a good driver.* By questioning the validity of the law, I decrease in my mind the authority of the law.

For that reason Paul is quick to remind us, "the law is holy, and the command is holy and right and good" (7:12). The root word for *holy* is *hagios,* which means "different." God's commands are holy because they come from a different world, a different sphere, a different perspective.

In a sense the "Do Not Enter" sign on my forbidden alley was from a different sphere. Our city lawmakers' thoughts are not like my thoughts. They are concerned for the public good. I am concerned with personal convenience. They want what is best for the city. I want what is best for me. They know what is safe. I know what is quick. But they don't create laws for my pleasure; they make laws for my safety.

The same is true with God. What we consider shortcuts God sees as disasters. He doesn't give laws for our pleasure. He gives them for our protection. In seasons of struggle we must trust his wisdom, not ours. He designed the system; he knows what we need.

But since I am stubborn, I think *I* do. My disrespect for the "Do Not Enter" sign reveals an ugly, selfish side of me. Had I never seen the law, I would have never seen how selfish I am.

A poignant example of this was penned seventeen hundred years ago by Augustine in his book *Confessions*:

> There was a pear tree near our vineyard, laden with fruit. One stormy night we rascally youths set out to rob it and carry our spoils away. We took off a huge load of pears—not to feast upon ourselves, but to throw them to the pigs, though we ate just enough to have the pleasure of forbidden fruit. They were nice pears, but it was not the pears that my wretched soul coveted for I had plenty better at home. I picked them simply in order to become a thief . . . the desire to steal was simply awakened by the prohibition of stealing.[1]

Augustine wasn't lured by the pears; he was lured by the fence. Isn't there within each of us a voice which says, "I wonder how many pears I can pick without being seen. I wonder how many times I can go down this one-way street without getting caught"?

The moment we begin asking those questions we have crossed an invisible line into the arena of fear. Grace delivered us from fear, but watch how quickly we return. Grace told us we didn't have to spend our lives looking over our shoulders, but look at us glancing backward. Grace told us that we were free from guilt, but look at us with pear stains on our cheeks and guilt on our consciences.

Don't we know better? What has happened to us? Why are we so quick to revert back to our old ways? Or as Paul so candidly writes, "What a miserable man I am! Who will save me from this body that brings me death?" (Rom. 7:24).

Simply stated: We are helpless to battle sin alone. Aren't we glad Paul answered his own question?

"I thank God for saving me through Jesus Christ our Lord!" (v. 25).

The same One who saved us first is there to save us still.

There is never a point at which you are any less saved than you were the first moment he saved you. Just because you were grumpy at breakfast doesn't mean you were condemned at breakfast. When you lost your temper yesterday, you didn't lose your salvation. Your name doesn't disappear and reappear in the book of life according to your moods and actions. Such is the message of grace. "There is now no condemnation for those who are in Christ Jesus" (Rom. 8:1 NIV).

You are saved, not because of what you do, but because of what Christ did. And you are special, not because of what you do, but because of whose you are. And you are his.

And because we are his, let's forget the shortcuts and stay on the main road. He knows the way. He drew the map. He knows the way home.

15	# The Heaviness of Hatred

Matthew
18:21–35

*Be kind and loving to each other, and for-
give each other just as God forgave you in
Christ.* EPHESIANS 4:32

Each week Kevin Tunell is required to mail a
dollar to a family he'd rather forget. They
sued him for $1.5 million but settled for $936,
to be paid a dollar at a time. The family
expects the payment each Friday so Tunell
won't forget what happened on the first Friday
of 1982.

That's the day their daughter was killed.
Tunell was convicted of manslaughter and
drunken driving. He was seventeen. She was
eighteen. Tunell served a court sentence. He
also spent seven years campaigning against
drunk driving, six years more than his sentence required. But he keeps forgetting to
send the dollar.

The weekly restitution is to last until the

year 2000. Eighteen years. Tunell makes the check out to the victim, mails it to her family, and the money is deposited in a scholarship fund.

The family has taken him to court four times for failure to comply. After the most recent appearance, Tunell spent thirty days in
jail. He insists that he's not defying the order but rather is haunted
by the girl's death and tormented by the reminders. He offered the
family two boxes of checks covering the payments until the year
2001, one year more than required. They refused. It's not money
they seek, but penance.

Quoting the mother, "We want to receive the check every week
on time. He must understand we are going to pursue this until
August of the year 2000. We will go back to court every month if
we have to."[1]

Few would question the anger of the family. Only the naive
would think it fair to leave the guilty unpunished. But I do have
one concern. Is 936 payments enough? Not for Tunell to send,
mind you, but for the family to demand? When they receive the
final payment, will they be at peace? In August 2000, will the family be able to put the matter to rest? Is eighteen years' worth of
restitution sufficient? Will 196 months' worth of remorse be adequate?

How much is enough? Were you in the family and were Tunell
your target, how many payments would you require? Better stated,
how many payments *do* you require?

No one—I repeat, *no one*—makes it through life free of injury.
Someone somewhere has hurt you. Like the eighteen-year-old,
you've been a victim. She died because someone drank too much.
Part of you has died because someone spoke too much, demanded
too much, or neglected too much.

The Habit of Hatred

Everyone gets wounded; hence everyone must decide: how many payments will I demand? We may not require that the offender write checks, but we have other ways of settling the score.

Silence is a popular technique. (Ignore them when they speak.) *Distance* is equally effective. (When they come your way, walk the other.) *Nagging* is a third tool for revenge. ("Oh, I see you still have fingers on your hand. Funny you never use them to dial my number." "Oh, Joe, nice of you to drop in on us *unpromoted* peons.")

Amazing how creative we can be at getting even. If I can soil one evening, spoil one day, foil one Friday, then justice is served and I'm content.

For now. Until I think of you again. Until I see you again. Until something happens that brings to mind the deed you did, then I'll demand another check. I'm not about to let you heal before I do. As long as I suffer, you suffer. As long as I hurt, you hurt. You cut me, and I'm going to make you feel bad as long as I bleed, even if I have to reopen the wound myself.

Call it a bad addiction. We start the habit innocently enough, indulging our hurts with doses of anger. Not much, just a needle or two of rancor. The rush numbs the hurt, so we come back for more and up the dosage; we despise not only what he did, but who he is. Insult him. Shame him. Ridicule him. The surge energizes. Drugged on malice, the roles are reversed; we aren't the victim, we're the victor. It feels good. Soon we hate him and anyone like him. ("All men are jerks." "Every preacher is a huckster." "You can't trust a woman.") The progression is predictable. Hurt becomes hate, and hate becomes rage as we become junkies unable to make it through the day without mainlining on bigotry and bitterness.

How will the score be settled? How do I break the cycle? How many payments do I demand? Peter had a similar question for Jesus: "Master, how many times do I forgive a brother or sister who hurts me? Seven?" (Matt. 18:21 MSG).

Peter is worried about over-forgiving an offender. The Jewish law stipulated that the wounded forgive three times. Peter is willing to double that and throw in one more for good measure. No doubt he thinks Jesus will be impressed. Jesus isn't. The Master's answer still stuns us. "Seven! Hardly. Try seventy times seven" (v. 22 MSG).

If you're pausing to multiply seventy times seven, you're missing the point. Keeping tabs on your mercy, Jesus is saying, is not being merciful. If you're calibrating your grace, you're not being gracious. There should never be a point when our grace is exhausted.

The Cause of Hatred

By this point Jesus' listeners are thinking of the Kevin Tunells in the world. "But what about the father who abandoned me as a kid?"

"And my wife who dumped me for a newer model?"

"And the boss who laid me off even though my child was sick?"

The Master silences them with a raised hand and the story of the forgetful servant.

The kingdom of heaven is like a king who decided to collect the money his servants owed him. When the king began to collect his money, a servant who owed several million dollars was brought to him. But the servant did not have enough money to pay the master, the king. So the master ordered that everything the servant owned should be sold, even the servant's wife and children. Then the money would be used to pay the king what the servant owed.

But the servant fell on his knees and begged, "Be patient with me, and I will pay you everything I owe." The master felt sorry for his servant and told him he did not have to pay it back. Then he let the servant go free. (Matt. 18:23–28)

This servant had a serious problem. Somehow he had amassed a bill worth millions of dollars. If he could pay a thousand dollars a day for thirty years, he'd be debt free. Fat chance. He didn't make a grand a day. His debt was far greater than his power to repay.

And unless you skipped the first half of this book, you know the same is true of us. Our debt is far greater than our power to repay.

Our pockets are empty while our debt is millions. We don't need a salary; we need a gift. We don't need swimming lessons; we need a lifeguard. We don't need a place to work; we need someone to work in our place. That "someone" is Jesus Christ. "God makes people right with himself through their faith in Jesus Christ. . . . God gave him as a way to forgive sin through faith in the blood of Jesus' death" (Rom. 3:22, 25).

Our Master has forgiven an insurmountable debt. Does God demand reimbursement? Does he insist on his pound of flesh? When your feet walk the wrong road, does he demand that you cut them off? When your eyes look twice where they should never look once, does he blind you? When you use your tongue for profanity instead of praise, does he cut it out?

If he did, we would be one maimed civilization. He demands no payment, at least not from us.

And those promises we make, "Just get me through this mess, God. I'll never disappoint you again." We're as bad as the debtor. "Be patient with me," he pledged. "I will pay you everything I owe." The thought of pleading for mercy never entered his mind. But though he never even begs for grace, he receives it. He leaves the king's chamber a debt-free man.

But he doesn't believe it.

Later, that same servant found another servant who owed him a few dollars. The servant grabbed him around the neck and said, "Pay me the money you owe me!"

The other servant fell on his knees and begged him, "Be patient with me, and I will pay you everything I owe."

But the first servant refused to be patient. He threw the other servant into prison until he could pay everything he owed. (Matt.
18:28–29)

Something is wrong with this picture. Are these the actions of a
man forgiven millions? Choking a person who owes him a few
bucks? Are these the words of a man who has been set free? "Pay
me the money you owe me!"

Remember the finger-pointer from the parable at the beginning
of the book? Here he is! So occupied with the mistake of his
brother that he misses the grace of the Father.

He demands that his debtor be put in jail until he can repay the
debt. How bizarre! Not only is he ungrateful, he is irrational. How
can he expect the man to earn money while in prison? If he has no
funds out of jail, will he discover some money in jail? Of course
not. What's he going to do? Sell magazines to the inmates? The
decision makes no sense.

But hatred never does.

How could this happen? How can one forgiven not forgive? How
could a free man not be quick to free others?

Part of the answer is found in the words of Jesus. "The person
who is forgiven only a little will love only a little" (Luke 7:47).

To believe we are totally and eternally debt free is seldom easy.
Even if we've stood before the throne and heard it from the king
himself, we still doubt. As a result, many are forgiven only a little,
not because the grace of the king is limited, but because the faith
of the sinner is small. God is willing to forgive all. He's willing to
wipe the slate completely clean. He guides us to a pool of mercy
and invites us to bathe. Some plunge in, but others just touch the
surface. They leave feeling unforgiven.

Apparently that was the problem of the servant. He still *felt* in
debt. How else can we explain his behavior? Rather than forgive

his transgressor, he chokes him! "I'll squeeze it out of you." He hates the very sight of the man. Why? Because the man owes him so much? I don't think so. He hates the man because the man reminds him of his debt to the master.

The king forgave the debt, but the servant never truly accepted the grace of the king. Now we understand why the Hebrew writer insisted, "See to it that no one misses the grace of God and that no bitter root grows up to cause trouble and defile many" (Heb. 12:15 NIV).

The Cure for Hatred

Where the grace of God is missed, bitterness is born. But where the grace of God is embraced, forgiveness flourishes. In what many believe to be Paul's final letter, he urges Timothy to "be strong in the grace we have in Christ Jesus" (2 Tim. 2:1).

How insightful is this last exhortation. Paul doesn't urge Timothy to be strong in prayer or Bible study or benevolence, as vital as each may be. He wants his son in the faith to major in grace. Claim *this* territory. Dwell on *this* truth. If you miss anything, don't miss the grace of God.

The longer we walk in the garden, the more likely we are to smell like flowers. The more we immerse ourselves in grace, the more likely we are to give grace. Could this be the clue for coping with anger? Could it be the secret is not in demanding payment but in pondering the payment of your Savior?

Your friend broke his promises? Your boss didn't keep her word? I'm sorry, but before you take action, answer this question: How did God react when you broke your promises to him?

You've been lied to? It hurts to be deceived. But before you double your fists, think: How did God respond when you lied to him?

You've been neglected? Forgotten? Left behind? Rejection hurts. But before you get even, get honest with yourself. Have you ever neglected God? Have you always been attentive to his will? None of us have. How did he react when you neglected him?

The key to forgiving others is to quit focusing on what they did to you and start focusing on what God did for you.

But, Max, that's not fair! Somebody has to pay for what he did.

I agree. Someone must pay, and Someone already has.

You don't understand, Max, this guy doesn't deserve grace. He doesn't deserve mercy. He's not worthy of forgiveness.

I'm not saying he is. But are you?

Besides, what other choice do you have? Hatred? The alternative is not appealing. Look what happens when we refuse to forgive, "The master was very angry and put the servant in prison to be punished until he could pay everything he owed" (Matt. 18:34).

Unforgiving servants always end up in prison. Prisons of anger, guilt, and depression. God doesn't have to put us in a jail; we create our own. "Some men stay healthy till the day they die . . . others have no happiness at all; they live and die with bitter hearts" (Job 21:23–25 TEV).

Oh, the gradual grasp of hatred. Its damage begins like the crack in my windshield. Thanks to a speeding truck on a gravel road, my window was chipped. With time the nick became a crack, and the crack became a winding tributary. Soon the windshield was a spider web of fragments. I couldn't drive my car without thinking of the jerk who drove too fast. Though I've never seen him, I could describe him. He is some deadbeat bum who cheats on his wife, drives with a six-pack on the seat, and keeps the television so loud the neighbors can't sleep. His carelessness blocked my vision. (Didn't do much for my view out the windshield either.)

Ever heard the expression "blind rage"?

Let me be very clear. Hatred will sour your outlook and break your back. The load of bitterness is simply too heavy. Your knees will buckle under the strain, and your heart will break beneath the weight. The mountain before you is steep enough without the heaviness of hatred on your back. The wisest choice—the *only* choice—is for you to drop the anger. You will never be called upon to give anyone more grace than God has already given you.

During World War I, a German soldier plunged into an out-of-the-way shell hole. There he found a wounded enemy. The fallen soldier was soaked with blood and only minutes from death. Touched by the plight of the man, the German soldier offered him water. Through this small kindness a bond was developed. The dying man pointed to his shirt pocket; the German soldier took from it a wallet and removed some family pictures. He held them so the wounded man could gaze at his loved ones one final time. With bullets raging over them and war all around them, these two enemies were, but for a few moments, friends.

What happened in that shell hole? Did all evil cease? Were all wrongs made right? No. What happened was simply this: Two enemies saw each other as humans in need of help. This is forgiveness. Forgiveness begins by rising above the war, looking beyond the uniform, and choosing to see the other, not as a foe or even as a friend, but simply as a fellow fighter longing to make it home safely.

16

Life Aboard the Fellow-Ship

Romans 15:7

*Welcome with open arms fellow believers
who don't see things the way you do.*
ROMANS 14:1 MSG

*Accept one another, then, just as Christ
accepted you, in order to bring praise to
God.* ROMANS 15:7 NIV

Grace makes three proclamations.

First, only God can forgive my godlessness. "Only God can forgive sins" (Mark 2:7). Dealing with my sins is God's responsibility. I repent, I confess, but only God can forgive. (And he does.)

Second, only God can judge my neighbor. "You cannot judge another person's servant. The master decides if the servant is doing well or not" (Rom. 14:4). Dealing with my neighbor is God's responsibility. I must speak; I must pray. But only God can convince. (And he does.)

Third, I must accept who God accepts. "Christ accepted you, so you should accept each other, which will bring glory to God"

(Rom. 15:7). God loves me and makes me his child. God loves my neighbor and makes him my brother. My privilege is to complete the triangle, to close the circuit by loving who God loves.

Easier said than done. "To live above with those we love, oh, how that will be glory. To live below with those we know, now that's another story."[1] Best I can figure the situation reads something like this . . .

Rocking the Boat

God has enlisted us in his navy and placed us on his ship. The boat has one purpose—to carry us safely to the other shore.

This is no cruise ship; it's a battleship. We aren't called to a life of leisure; we are called to a life of service. Each of us has a different task. Some, concerned with those who are drowning, are snatching people from the water. Others are occupied with the enemy, so they man the cannons of prayer and worship. Still others devote themselves to the crew, feeding and training the crew members.

Though different, we are the same. Each can tell of a personal encounter with the captain, for each has received a personal call. He found us among the shanties of the seaport and invited us to follow him. Our faith was born at the sight of his fondness, and so we went.

We each followed him across the gangplank of his grace onto the same boat. There is one captain and one destination. Though the battle is fierce, the boat is safe, for our captain is God. The ship will not sink. For that, there is no concern.

There is concern, however, regarding the disharmony of the crew. When we first boarded we assumed the crew was made up of others like us. But as we've wandered these decks, we've encountered curious converts with curious appearances. Some wear uni-forms we've never seen, sporting styles we've never witnessed. "Why do you look the way you do?" we ask them.

"Funny," they reply. "We were about to ask the same of you."

The variety of dress is not nearly as disturbing as the plethora of opinions. There is a group, for example, who clusters every morn-ing for serious study. They promote rigid discipline and somber expressions. "Serving the captain is serious business," they explain. It's no coincidence that they tend to congregate around the stern.

There is another regiment deeply devoted to prayer. Not only do they believe in prayer, they believe in prayer by kneeling. For that reason you always know where to locate them; they are at the bow of the ship.

And then there are a few who staunchly believe real wine should be used in the Lord's Supper. You'll find them on the port side.

Still another group has positioned themselves near the engine. They spend hours examining the nuts and bolts of the boat. They've been known to go below deck and not come up for days. They are occasionally criticized by those who linger on the top deck, feeling the wind in their hair and the sun on their face. "It's not what you learn," those topside argue. "It's what you feel that matters."

And, oh, how we tend to cluster.

Some think once you're on the boat, you can't get off. Others say you'd be foolish to go overboard, but the choice is yours.

Some believe you volunteer for service; others believe you were destined for the service before the ship was even built.

Some predict a storm of great tribulation will strike before we dock; others say it won't hit until we are safely ashore.

There are those who speak to the captain in a personal language. There are those who think such languages are extinct.

There are those who think the officers should wear robes, there are those who think there should be no officers at all, and there are those who think we are all officers and should all wear robes.

And, oh, how we tend to cluster.

And then there is the issue of the weekly meeting at which the captain is thanked and his words are read. All agree on its importance, but few agree on its nature. Some want it loud, others quiet. Some want ritual, others spontaneity. Some want to celebrate so they can meditate; others meditate so they can celebrate. Some want a meeting for those who've gone overboard. Others want to reach those overboard but without going overboard and neglecting those on board.

And, oh, how we tend to cluster.

The consequence is a rocky boat. There is trouble on deck. Fights have broken out. Sailors have refused to speak to each other. There have even been times when one group refused to acknowledge the presence of others on the ship. Most tragically, some adrift at sea have chosen not to board the boat because of the quarreling of the sailors.

"What do we do?" we'd like to ask the captain. "How can there be harmony on the ship?" We don't have to go far to find the answer.

On the last night of his life Jesus prayed a prayer that stands as a citadel for all Christians:

> I pray for these followers, but I am also praying for all those who will believe in me because of their teaching. Father, I pray that they can be one. As you are in me and I am in you, I pray that they can also be one in us. Then the world will believe that you sent me. (John 17:20)

How precious are these words. Jesus, knowing the end is near, prays one final time for his followers. Striking, isn't it, that he prayed not for their success, their safety, or their happiness.

He prayed for their unity. He prayed that they would love each other.

As he prayed for them, he also prayed for "those who will believe because of their teaching." That means us! In his last prayer Jesus prayed that you and I be one.

The Command of Acceptance

Of all the lessons we can draw from this verse, don't miss the most important: Unity matters to God. The Father does not want his kids to squabble. Disunity disturbs him. Why? Because "all people will know that you are my followers if you love each other" (John 13:35). Unity creates belief. How will the world believe that Jesus was sent by God? Not if we agree with each other. Not if we solve every controversy. Not if we are unanimous on each vote. Not if we never make a doctrinal error. But if we love one another.

Unity creates belief. Disunity fosters disbelief. Who wants to board a ship of bickering sailors? Life on the ocean may be rough, but at least the waves don't call us names.

Paul Billheimer may very well be right when he says:

> The continuous and widespread fragmentation of the Church has been the scandal of the ages. It has been Satan's master strategy. The sin of disunity probably has caused more souls to be lost than all other sins combined."[2]

"All people will know that you are my followers if you love each other." Stop and think about this verse for a minute. Could it be that *unity* is the key to reaching the world for Christ?

If unity is the key to evangelism, shouldn't it have precedence in our prayers? Shouldn't we, as Paul said, "make every effort to keep the unity of the Spirit through the bond of peace" (Eph. 4:3 NIV)? If unity matters to God, then shouldn't unity matter to us?

If unity is a priority in heaven, then shouldn't it be a priority on earth?

Nowhere, by the way, are we told to *build* unity. We are told simply to *keep* unity. From God's perspective there is but "one flock and one shepherd" (John 10:16). Unity does not need to be created; it simply needs to be protected.

How do we do that? How do we make every effort to keep the unity? Does that mean we compromise our convictions? No. Does that mean we abandon the truths we cherish? No. But it does mean we look long and hard at the attitudes we carry.

A Case Study in Capernaum

Sometime ago Denalyn bought a monkey. I didn't want a monkey in our house, so I objected.

"Where is he going to eat?" I asked.

"At our table."

"Where is he going to sleep?" I inquired.

"In our bed."

"What about the odor?" I demanded.

"I got used to you; I guess the monkey can too."

Unity doesn't begin in examining others but in examining self. Unity begins, not in demanding that others change, but in admitting that we aren't so perfect ourselves.

For a great example of this, go to a village called Capernaum and enter a small house occupied by Jesus and the disciples. Listen as the Master asks them a question. "What were you arguing about on the road?" (Mark 9:33).

The disciples' faces flush, not red with anger but pink with embarrassment. They had argued. About doctrine? No. Over strategy? Not that either. Ethics and values? Sorry. They had argued about which of them was the greatest.

Peter thought he was (he'd walked on water). John laid claim to the top slot (he was Jesus' favorite). Matthew boasted he was the best (after all, his book would be first in the New Testament). Power plays and one-upmanship. Is that where division usually begins?

> Where jealousy and selfishness are, there will be confusion and every kind of evil. (James 3:16)
>
> Do you know where your fights and arguments come from? They come from the selfish desires that wage war within you. (James 4:1)

Remarkable. Jockeying for position in the very presence of Christ. But not as remarkable as Jesus' response to them.

"Whoever *accepts* a child like this in my name *accepts* me. And whoever *accepts* me *accepts* the One who sent me" (Mark 9:37 italics mine).

Jesus felt so strongly about acceptance that he used the word four times in one sentence.

The answer to arguments? Acceptance. The first step to unity? Acceptance. Not agreement, acceptance. Not unanimity, acceptance. Not negotiation, arbitration, or elaboration. Those might come later but only after the first step, acceptance.

Such an answer troubles John. Too simplistic. The Son of Thunder was unacquainted with tolerance. Why, you just don't go around "accepting" people! Fences have to be built. Boundaries are a necessary part of religion. Case in point? John has one.

The Test of Divergence

"Teacher, we saw someone using your name to force demons out of a person. We told him to stop, because he does not belong to our group" (Mark 9:38).

John has a dilemma. He and the other disciples ran into

someone who was doing great work. This man was casting out
demons (the very act the disciples had trouble doing in Mark
9:20). He was changing lives. And, what's more, the man was giving the credit to God. He was doing it in the name of Christ.

Everything about him was so right. Right results. Right heart.
But there was one problem. He was from the wrong group.

So the disciples did what any able-bodied religious person would
do with someone from the wrong group. They escorted him to the
hull of the boat and put him in confinement. "We told him to stop,
because he does not belong to our group" (v. 38).

John wants to know if they did the right thing. John's not cocky;
he's confused. So are many people today. What do you do about
good things done in another group? What do you do when you like
the fruit but not the orchard?

I've asked that question. I am deeply appreciative of my heritage.
It was through a small, West Texas Church of Christ that I came to
know the Nazarene, the cross, and the Word. The congregation
wasn't large, maybe two hundred on a good Sunday. Most of the
families were like mine, blue-collar oil-field workers. But it was a
loving church. When our family was sick, the members visited us.
When we were absent, they called. And when this prodigal
returned, they embraced me.

I deeply appreciate my heritage. But through the years, my faith
has been supplemented by people of other groups. I wasn't long on
God's ship before I found encouragement in other staterooms.

A Brazilian Pentecostal taught me about prayer. A British
Anglican by the name of C. S. Lewis put muscle in my faith. A
Southern Baptist helped me understand grace.

One Presbyterian, Steve Brown, taught me about God's sover-
eignty while another, Frederick Buechner, taught me about God's
passion. A Catholic, Brennan Manning, convinced me that Jesus is
relentlessly tender. I'm a better husband because I read James

Dobson and a better preacher because I listened to Chuck Swindoll and Bill Hybels.

And only when I get home will I learn the name of a radio preacher whose message steered me back to Christ. I was a graduate student who'd lost his bearings. Needing some money over Christmas break, I took a job driving an oil-field delivery truck. The radio only picked up one station. A preacher was preaching. On a cold December day in 1978 I heard him describe the cross. I don't know his name. I don't know his heritage. He could have been a Quaker or an angel or both for all I know. But something about what he said caused me to pull the pickup onto the side of the road and rededicate my life to Christ.

Examine the Fruit and the Faith

What do you do when you see great works done by folks of other groups? Not divisive acts, not heretical teachings, but good works that give glory to God? Let's return to the conversation between Jesus and the disciples.

Before you note what Jesus said to John, note what he didn't say.

Jesus did not say, "John, if the people are nice, they are in." Generous gestures and benevolent acts are not necessarily a sign of a disciple. Just because a group is distributing toys at Christmas doesn't mean they are Christians. Just because they are feeding the hungry does not mean they are the honored ones of God. Jesus doesn't issue a call for blind tolerance.

Nor does he endorse blanket rejection. If unanimity of opinion were necessary for fellowship, this would have been a perfect time for Jesus to say so. But he didn't. Jesus didn't hand John a book of regulations by which to measure every candidate. Were such a checklist necessary, this would have been the ideal time to give it. But he didn't.

Look at what Jesus did say: "Don't stop him, because anyone who uses my name to do powerful things will not easily say evil things about me" (Mark 9:39).

Jesus was impressed with the man's *pure faith* (". . . who uses my name") and his *powerful fruit* (". . . to do powerful things"). His answer offers us a crucial lesson on studied tolerance. How should you respond to a good heart from a different religious heritage?

First, look at the fruit. Is it good? Is it healthy? Is he or she helping or hurting people? Production is more important than pedigree. The fruit is more important than the name of the orchard. If the person is bearing fruit, be grateful! A good tree cannot produce bad fruit (see Matt. 7:17), so be thankful that God is at work in other groups than yours.

But also look at the faith. In whose name is the work done? Jesus was accepting of this man's work because it was done in the name of Christ. What does it mean to do something "in the name of Jesus"? It means you are under the authority of and empowered by that name.

If I go to a car dealership and say I want a free car, the salespeople are going to laugh at me. If, however, I go with a letter written and signed by the owner of the dealership granting me a free car, then I drive off in a free car. Why? Because I am there under the authority of and empowered by the owner.

The Master says examine the person's faith. If he or she has faith in Jesus and is empowered by God, grace says that's enough. This is an important point. There are some who do not work in God's name. Remember the rock-stackers and the finger-pointers in the parable? They present a salvation of works rather than a salvation of grace. They are not working in the name of God, indeed they do not need God. They are working under the banner of human-merit self-righteousness. Just as Paul was intolerant of self-salvation, we must be as well.

But there are believers in many different heritages who cast their hope in God's firstborn Son and put their faith in the cross of Christ. If they, like you, are trusting him to carry them to the father's castle, don't you share a common Savior? If their trust, like yours, is in the all-sufficient sacrifice of Christ, aren't you covered with the same grace?

You mean they don't have to be in my group? No.

They don't have to share my background? They don't.

They don't have to see everything the way I do? Does anyone?

What is important is their fruit and their faith. Later, a much more tempered Son of Thunder would reduce it to this. "Whoever confesses that Jesus is the Son of God has God living inside, and that person lives in God" (1 John 4:15).

Ironic. The one who challenged the simple answer of the Master eventually rendered the simplest answer himself.

It should be simple. Where there is faith, repentance, and a new birth, there is a Christian. When I meet a man whose faith is in the cross and whose eyes are on the Savior, I meet a brother. Wasn't that Paul's approach? When he wrote the church in Corinth, he addressed a body of Christians guilty of every sin from abusing the Lord's Supper to arguing over the Holy Spirit. But how does he address them? "I beg you, brothers and sisters" (1 Cor. 1:10).

When the church in Rome was debating whether to eat meat offered to idols, did Paul tell them to start two churches? One for the meat-eaters and one for the non-meat-eaters? No, on the contrary, he urged, "Christ accepted you, so you should accept each other, which will bring glory to God" (Rom. 15:7).

Is God asking us to do anything more than what he has already done? Hasn't he gone a long way in accepting us? If God can tolerate my mistakes, can't I tolerate the mistakes of others? If God allows me, with my foibles and failures, to call him Father, shouldn't I extend the same grace to others? In fact, who can offer grace except those secure in the grip of grace? If God doesn't demand perfection, should I?

"They are God's servants," Paul reminds us, "not yours. They are responsible to him, not to you. Let him tell them whether they are right or wrong. And God is able to make them do as they should" (Rom. 14:4 TLB).

God's ship is a grand vessel. Just as a ship has many rooms, so God's kingdom has room for many opinions. But just as a ship has one deck, God's kingdom has a common ground: the all-sufficient sacrifice of Jesus Christ.

Will you pray with me for the day when Jesus' prayer is answered?

Will you pray with me for the day when the world is won because the church is one?

Will you pray with me for the day when we come out of our rooms and stand together to salute our captain? When clusters cease and the chorus commences?

Jesus' final prayer before the cross was for the unity of his followers. Would he offer a prayer that couldn't be answered? I don't think so either.

17 | What We Really Want to Know

Romans 8:31–39

Can anything separate us from the love
Christ has for us?   ROMANS 8:35

It was her singing that did it. At first I didn't notice. Had no reason to. The circumstances were commonplace. A daddy picking up his six-year-old from a Brownie troop meeting. Sara loves Brownies; she loves the awards she earns and the uniform she wears. She'd climbed in the car and shown me her new badge and freshly baked cookie. I'd turned onto the road, turned on her favorite music, and turned my attention to more sophisticated matters of schedules and obligations.

But only steps into the maze of thought I stepped back out. Sara was singing. Singing about God. Singing to God. Head back, chin up, and lungs full, she filled the car with music. Heaven's harps paused to listen.

Is that my daughter? She sounds older. She looks older, taller, even prettier. Did I sleep through something? What happened to the chubby cheeks? What happened to the little face and pudgy fingers? She is becoming a young lady. Blonde hair down to her shoulders. Feet dangling over the seat. Somewhere in the night a page had turned and, well, look at her!

If you're a parent you know what I mean. Just yesterday diapers, today the car keys? Suddenly your child is halfway to the dormitory, and you're running out of chances to show your love, so you speak.

That's what I did. The song stopped and Sara stopped, and I ejected the tape and put my hand on her shoulder and said, "Sara, you're something special." She turned and smiled tolerantly. "Someday some hairy-legged boy is going to steal your heart and sweep you into the next century. But right now, you belong to me."

She tilted her head, looked away for a minute, then looked back and asked, "Daddy, why are you acting so weird?"

I suppose such words would sound strange to a six-year-old. The love of a parent falls awkwardly on the ears of a child. My burst of emotion was beyond her. But that didn't keep me from speaking.

There is no way our little minds can comprehend the love of God. But that didn't keep him from coming.

And we, too, have tilted our heads. Like Sara, we have wondered what our Father was doing. From the cradle in Bethlehem to the cross in Jerusalem, we've pondered the love of our Father. What *can* you say to that kind of emotion? Upon learning that God would rather die than live without you, how do you react? How can you begin to explain such passion? If you're Paul the apostle, you don't. You make no statements. You offer no explanations. You ask a few questions. Five questions, to be exact.

Paul's response to God's grace is a quintet of queries, launched like fireworks, not to bring answers, but to bring amazement. "[Paul] challenges anybody and everybody, in heaven, earth or hell, to answer them and deny the truth which they contain."[1]

These questions are not new to you. You've asked them. In the night you've asked them; in anger you've asked them. The doctor's diagnosis brought them to the surface, as did the court's decision and the phone call from the bank. The questions are probes of pain and problem and circumstance. No, the questions are not new, but maybe the answers are.

The Question of Protection

"If God is for us, who can be against us?" (Rom 8:31 NIV).

The question is not simply, "Who can be against us?" You could answer that one. Who is against you? Disease, inflation, corruption, exhaustion. Calamities confront, and fears imprison. Were Paul's question, "Who can be against us?" we could list our foes much easier than we could fight them. But that is not the question. The question is, *If GOD IS FOR US, who can be against us?*

Indulge me for a moment. Four words in this verse deserve your attention. Read slowly the phrase, "God is for us." Please pause for a minute before you continue. Read it again, aloud. (My apologies to the person next to you.) *God is for us.* Repeat the phrase four times, this time emphasizing each word. (Come on, you're not in that big of a hurry.)

God is for us.

God *is* for us.

God is *for* us.

God is for *us.*

God is for you. Your parents may have forgotten you, your teachers may have neglected you, your siblings may be ashamed of you;

but within reach of your prayers is the maker of the oceans. God!

God *is* for you. Not "may be," not "has been," not "was," not "would be," but "God is!" He *is* for you. Today. At this hour. At this minute. As you read this sentence. No need to wait in line or come back tomorrow. He is with you. He could not be closer than he is at this second. His loyalty won't increase if you are better nor lessen if you are worse. He *is* for you.

God is *for* you. Turn to the sidelines; that's God cheering your run. Look past the finish line; that's God applauding your steps. Listen for him in the bleachers, shouting your name. Too tired to continue? He'll carry you. Too discouraged to fight? He's picking you up. God is *for* you.

God is for *you*. Had he a calendar, your birthday would be circled. If he drove a car, your name would be on his bumper. If there's a tree in heaven, he's carved your name in the bark. We know he has a tattoo, and we know what it says. "I have written your name on my hand," he declares (Isa. 49:16).

"Can a mother forget the baby at her breast and have no compassion on the child she has borne?" God asks in Isaiah 49:15 (NIV). What a bizarre question. Can you mothers imagine feeding your infant and then later asking, "What was that baby's name?" No. I've seen you care for your young. You stroke the hair, you touch the face, you sing the name over and over. Can a mother forget? No way. But "even if she could forget, . . . I will not forget you," God pledges (Isa. 49:15).

God is with you. Knowing that, who is against you? Can death harm you now? Can disease rob your life? Can your purpose be taken or your value diminished? No. Though hell itself may set itself against you, no one can defeat you. You are protected. God is with you.

The Question of Provision

"He who did not spare his own Son, but gave him up for us all—how will he not also, along with him, graciously give us all things?" (Rom. 8:32 NIV).

Suppose a man comes upon a child being beaten by thugs. He dashes into the mob, rescues the boy, and carries him to a hospital. The youngster is nursed to health. The man pays for the child's treatment. He learns that the child is an orphan and adopts him as his own and gives the boy his name. And then, one night, months later, the father hears the son sobbing into his pillow. He goes to him and asks about the tears.

"I'm worried, Daddy. I'm worried about tomorrow. Where will I get food to eat? How am I going to buy clothes to stay warm? And where will I sleep?"

The father is rightfully troubled. "Haven't I shown you? Don't you understand? I risked my life to save you. I gave my money to treat you. You wear my name. I've called you my son. Would I do all that and then not meet your needs?"

This is Paul's question. *Would he who gave his Son not meet our needs?*

But still we worry. We worry about the IRS and the SAT and the FBI. We worry about education, recreation, and constipation. We worry that we won't have enough money, and when we have money we worry that we won't manage it well. We worry that the world will end before the parking meter expires. We worry what the dog thinks if he sees us step out of the shower. We worry that someday we'll learn that fat-free yogurt was fattening.

Honestly, now. Did God save you so you would fret? Would he teach you to walk just to watch you fall? Would he be nailed to the cross for your sins and then disregard your prayers? Come on. Is

Scripture teasing us when it reads, "He has put his angels in charge of you to watch over you wherever you go"? (Ps. 91:11)

I don't think so either.

Two Questions about Guilt and Grace

"Who can accuse the people God has chosen? No one, because God is the One who makes them right. Who can say God's people are guilty? No one, because Christ Jesus died, but he was also raised from the dead, and now he is on God's right side, begging God for us" (Rom. 8:33–34).

Sometime ago I read a story of a youngster who was shooting rocks with a slingshot. He could never hit his target. As he returned to Grandma's backyard, he spied her pet duck. On impulse he took aim and let fly. The stone hit, and the duck was dead. The boy panicked and hid the bird in the woodpile, only to look up and see his sister watching.

After lunch that day, Grandma told Sally to help with the dishes. Sally responded, "Johnny told me he wanted to help in the kitchen today. Didn't you Johnny?" And she whispered to him, "Remember the duck!" So, Johnny did the dishes.

What choice did he have? For the next several weeks he was at the sink often. Sometimes for his duty, sometimes for his sin. "Remember the duck," Sally'd whisper when he objected.

So weary of the chore, he decided that any punishment would be better than washing more dishes, so he confessed to killing the duck. "I know, Johnny," his grandma said, giving him a hug. "I was standing at the window and saw the whole thing. Because I love you, I forgave you. I wondered how long you would let Sally make a slave out of you."[2]

He'd been pardoned, but he thought he was guilty. Why? He had listened to the words of his accuser.

You have been accused as well. You have been accused of dishonesty. You've been accused of immorality. You've been accused of greed, anger, and arrogance.

Every moment of your life, your accuser is filing charges against you. He has noticed every error and marked each slip. Neglect your priorities, and he will jot it down. Abandon your promises, and he will make a note. Try to forget your past; he'll remind you. Try to undo your mistakes; he will thwart you.

This expert witness has no higher goal than to take you to court and press charges. Even his name, Diabolos, means "slanderer." Who is he? The devil.

He is "the accuser of our brothers and sisters, who accused them day and night before our God" (Rev. 12:10). Can't you see him? Pacing back and forth before God's bench. Can't you hear him? Calling your name, listing your faults.

He rails: "This one you call your child, God. He is not worthy. Greed lingers within. When he speaks, he thinks often of himself. He'll go days without an honest prayer. Why, even this morning he chose to sleep rather than spend time with you. I accuse him of laziness, egotism, worry, distrust . . ."

As he speaks, you hang your head. You have no defense. His charges are fair. "I plead guilty, your honor," you mumble.

"The sentence?" Satan asks.

"The wages of sin is death," explains the judge, "but in this case the death has already occurred. For this one died with Christ."

Satan is suddenly silent. And you are suddenly jubilant. You realize that Satan cannot accuse you. No one can accuse you! Fingers may point and voices may demand, but the charges glance off like arrows hitting a shield. No more dirty dishwater. No more penance. No more nagging sisters. You have stood before the judge and heard him declare, "Not guilty."

"The Lord GOD helps me, so I will not be ashamed. I will be

determined, and I know I will not be disgraced. He shows that I am innocent, and he is close to me. So who can accuse me? If there is someone, let us go to court together" (Isa. 50:7–8).

Once the judge has released you, you need not fear the court.

The Question of Endurance

"Can anything separate us from the love Christ has for us?" (Rom. 8:35).

There it is. This is the question. Here is what we want to know. We want to know how long God's love will endure. Paul could have begun with this one. Does God really love us forever? Not just on Easter Sunday when our shoes are shined and our hair is fixed. We want to know (deep within, don't we really want to know?), how does God feel about me when I'm a jerk? Not when I'm peppy and positive and ready to tackle world hunger. Not then. I know how he feels about me then. Even I like me then.

I want to know how he feels about me when I snap at anything that moves, when my thoughts are gutter-level, when my tongue is sharp enough to slice a rock. How does he feel about me then?

That's the question. That's the concern. That's the reason most of you read this book. Oh, you don't say it; you may not even know it. But I can see it on your faces. I can hear it in your words. Did I cross the line this week? Last Tuesday when I drank vodka until I couldn't walk . . . last Thursday when my business took me where I had no business being . . . last summer when I cursed the God who made me as I stood near the grave of the child he gave me?

Did I drift too far? Wait too long? Slip too much?

That's what we want to know.

Can anything separate us from the love Christ has for us?

God answered our question before we asked it. So we'd see his answer, he lit the sky with a star. So we'd hear it, he filled the night with a choir; and so we'd believe it, he did what no man had ever dreamed. He became flesh and dwelt among us.

He placed his hand on the shoulder of humanity and said, "You're something special."

Untethered by time, he sees us all. From the backwoods of Virginia to the business district of London; from the Vikings to the astronauts, from the cave-dwellers to the kings, from the hut-builders to the finger-pointers to the rock-stackers, he sees us. Vagabonds and ragamuffins all, he saw us before we were born.

And he loves what he sees. Flooded by emotion. Overcome by pride, the Starmaker turns to us, one by one, and says, "You are my child. I love you dearly. I'm aware that someday you'll turn from me and walk away. But I want you to know, I've already provided you a way back."

And to prove it, he did something extraordinary.

Stepping from the throne, he removed his robe of light and wrapped himself in skin: pigmented, human skin. The light of the universe entered a dark, wet womb. He who angels worship nestled himself in the placenta of a peasant, was birthed into the cold night, and then slept on cow's hay.

Mary didn't know whether to give him milk or give him praise, but she gave him both since he was, as near as she could figure, hungry and holy.

Joseph didn't know whether to call him Junior or Father. But in the end called him Jesus, since that's what the angel said and since he didn't have the faintest idea what to name a God he could cradle in his arms.

Neither Mary nor Joseph said it as bluntly as my Sara, but don't you think their heads tilted and their minds wondered, "What in the world are you doing, God?" Or, better phrased, "God, what are you doing in the world?"

"Can anything make me stop loving you?" God asks. "Watch me

speak your language, sleep on your earth, and feel your hurts. Behold the maker of sight and sound as he sneezes, coughs, and blows his nose. You wonder if I understand how you feel? Look into the dancing eyes of the kid in Nazareth; that's God walking to school. Ponder the toddler at Mary's table; that's God spilling his milk.

"You wonder how long my love will last? Find your answer on a splintered cross, on a craggy hill. That's me you see up there, your maker, your God, nail-stabbed and bleeding. Covered in spit and sin-soaked. That's your sin I'm feeling. That's your death I'm dying. That's your resurrection I'm living. That's how much I love you."

"Can anything come between you and me?" asks the firstborn Son.

Hear the answer and stake your future on the triumphant words of Paul: "I am sure that neither death, nor life, nor angels, nor ruling spirits, nothing now, nothing in the future, no powers, nothing above us, nothing below us, nor anything else in the whole world will ever be able to separate us from the love of God that is in Christ Jesus our Lord" (Rom. 8:38–39).

Conclusion
"Don't Forget to Look After Me"

"Good, I'm glad you're sitting by me. Sometimes I throw up."

Not exactly what you like to hear from the airline passenger in the next seat. Before I had time to store my bag in the overhead compartment, I knew his name, age, and itinerary. "I'm Billy Jack. I'm fourteen, and I'm going home to see my daddy." I started to tell him my name, but he spoke first.

"I need someone to look after me. I get confused a lot."

He told me about the special school he attended and the medication he took. "Can you remind me to take my pill in a few minutes?" Before we buckled up he stopped the airline attendant. "Don't forget about me," he told her. "I get confused."

Once we were airborne, Billy Jack ordered a soft drink and dipped his pretzels in it. He kept glancing at me as I drank and asked if he could drink what I didn't. He spilled some of his soda and apologized.

"No problem," I said, wiping it up.

Billy Jack showed me his cassette player and asked if I'd like to listen to one of his tapes. "I brought my favorites," he smiled, handing me the sound tracks from *The Little Mermaid*, *Aladdin*, and *The Lion King*.

When he started playing with his Nintendo Game Boy, I tried to doze off. That's when he started making noises with his mouth, imitating a trumpet. "I can sound like the ocean, too," he bragged, swishing spit back and forth in his cheeks.

(Didn't sound like the ocean, but I didn't tell him.)

Billy Jack was a little boy in a big body. "Can clouds hit the ground?" he asked me. I started to answer, but he looked back out the window like he'd never asked. Unashamed of his needs, he didn't let a flight attendant pass without a reminder: "Don't forget to look after me."

When they brought the food: "Don't forget to look after me."

When they brought more drinks: "Don't forget to look after me."

When any attendant would pass, Billy Jack would urge: "Don't forget to look after me."

I honestly can't think of one time Billy Jack didn't remind the crew that he needed attention. The rest of us didn't. We never asked for help. We were grownups. Sophisticated. Self-reliant. Seasoned travelers. Most of us didn't even listen to the emergency landing instructions. (Billy Jack asked me to explain them to him.)

Midway through the writing of this book I remembered Billy Jack. He would have understood the idea of grace. He knew what it was like to place himself totally in the care of someone else. I didn't share with him "The Parable of the River" (it wasn't written yet), but I know which brother he would have liked.

The youngest. The one who let the elder brother carry him up the river. He wouldn't have understood the three who refused the offer of the firstborn son. Why *not* place your care in the hands of someone stronger?

Have you?

Many haven't. We are sophisticated, mature. An epistle to challenge the self-sufficient, Romans was written for folks like us. Confession of need is admission of weakness, something we are slow to do. That's why I think Billy Jack would have understood grace. It occurred to me that he was the safest person on the flight. Had the plane encountered trouble, he would have received primary assistance. The flight attendants would have bypassed me and gone to him. Why? He had placed himself in the care of someone stronger.

Again I ask, have you?

One thing's for sure: You cannot save yourself. The river is too strong; the distance is too great. God has sent his firstborn Son to carry you home. Are you firmly in the grip of his grace? I pray that you are. I *earnestly* pray that you are.

Before we conclude our time together, would you spend some time with the following questions? May the Holy Spirit use them to reveal any resistance you might have to God's grace.

Are you quick to tell others of the rocks you've stacked? Or do you prefer boasting about the strength of your elder brother?

Do you live in fear of never doing enough? Or do you live in gratitude, knowing enough has already been done?

Do you have a small circle, accepting only the few who work like you? Or do you have a large circle, accepting all who love who you love?

Do you worship to impress God? Or do you worship to thank God?

Do you do good deeds in order to be saved? Or do you do good deeds because you are saved?

Do you pray, "God, I thank you that I am not like other people who steal, cheat, or take part in adultery"?[1]

Or do you confess, "God, have mercy on me, a sinner"?

* * *

One last thought. Billy Jack spent the final hour of the flight with his head on my shoulder, his hands folded between his knees. Just when I thought he was asleep, his head popped up and he said, "My dad is going to meet me at the airport. I can't wait to see him because he watches after me."

Paul would have liked Billy Jack.

Notes

INTRODUCTION

1. Edward Mote, "The Solid Rock."
2. Martin Luther, "Preface to the Epistle of St. Paul to the Romans," *Luther's Works*, vol. 35, ed. J. Pelikan and H. Lehmann: Muhlenburg Press, 1960), page 365.

CHAPTER 2 GOD'S GRACIOUS ANGER

1. Anders Nygren, *Commentary on Romans*, (Philadelphia: Fortress Press, 1949), 98.
2. Carthaginian theologian Tertullian, quoted in William Barclay, *The Letter to the Romans*, (Louisville, Ky.: Westminster Press, 1975, 27.

CHAPTER 3 GODLESS LIVING

1. Ravi Zacharias, *Can Man Live Without God?* (Dallas: Word, 1994), 23.
2. Stephen Jay Gould, quoted in Donald McCullough, *The Trivialization of God* (Colorado Springs: NavPress, 1995), 16.

CHAPTER 4 GODLESS JUDGING

1. John Stott, *Romans: God's Good News for the World* (Downers Grove, IL: InterVarsity Press, 1994), 82.

CHAPTER 5 GODLESS RELIGION

1. From "Definition of Justification," in Richard Hooker's *Ecclesiastical Policy*, as quoted in Stott, *Romans: God's Good News for the World*, 118.

CHAPTER 6 CALLING THE CORPSES

1. Dr. Li Zhisui, "The Private Life of Chairman Mao," *US News and World Report*, 10 October 1994, 55–90.

CHAPTER 7 WHERE LOVE AND JUSTICE MEET

1. Stott, *Romans: God's Good News for the World*, 112.
2. Ibid., 118.
3. John MacArthur, *The New Testament Commentary of Romans* (Chicago: Moody 1991, 199.

CHAPTER 8 CREDIT WHERE CREDIT IS NOT DUE

1. Dr. Leon Morris, *The Epistle to the Romans* (Grand Rapids, Mich.: Eerdmans and InterVarsity, 1988), as quoted in Stott, *Romans: God's Good News for the World*, 109.

CHAPTER 9 MAJOR LEAGUE GRACE

1. I heard this story at a ministers retreat featuring Gordon MacDonald in February 1990.

CHAPTER 10 THE PRIVILEGE OF PAUPERS

1. Dr. Paul Faulkner, *Achieving Success without Failing Your Family* (W. Monroe La.: Howard Publishing, 1994), 14–15.
2. *1041 Sermon Illustrations, Ideas and Expositions* (Grand Rapids, Mich.: Baker, 1953), 244.
3. Charles R. Swindoll, *The Grace Awakening* (Waco, Tex.: Word, 1990), 70.

CHAPTER 11 GRACE WORKS

1. Charles Colson, "Making the World Safe for Religion," *Christianity Today*, 8 November 1993, 33.
2. Stott, *Romans: God's Good News for the World*, 169.
3. William Sanday and Arthur C. Headlam, "A Critical and Exegetical Commentary on the Epistle to the Romans," in the *The International Commentary*.

CHAPTER 13 SUFFICIENT GRACE

1. Max Lucado, *God Came Near* (Portland, Oreg.: Multnomah Press, 1987), 151–52.

CHAPTER 14 THE CIVIL WAR OF THE SOUL

1. Augustine, *Confessions*, as quoted by William Barclay, *The Letter to the Romans* (Philadelphia: Westminster Press, 1977), 98.

CHAPTER 15 THE HEAVINESS OF HATRED
1. "Drunken Driver Skips $1 Weekly Payments to Victim's Parents," *San Antonio Light*, 31 March 1990.

CHAPTER 16 LIFE ABOARD THE FELLOW-SHIP
1. Source unknown.
2. Paul Billheimer, *Love Covers* (Minneapolis: Bethany House, 1981), 7.

CHAPTER 17 WHAT WE REALLY WANT TO KNOW
1. Stott, *Romans: God's Good News for the World*, 254.
2. Steven Cole, "Forgiveness," *Leadership Magazine*, 1983, 86.

CONCLUSION: "DON'T FORGET TO LOOK AFTER ME"
1. Luke 18:11–13.

Study Guide
Written by Steve Halliday

Each of these short studies is designed not only to help you think through and apply the ideas developed in *In The Grip Of Grace*, but also to help you interact with the biblical passages that prompted those ideas.

The first section of each study, "Looking Back," excerpts portions of each chapter and supplies questions for personal or group study. The second section, "Looking Deep," helps you dig a little deeper into Scripture's perspective on the topic under discussion.

Introduction:

The Greatest Discovery of My Life

Looking Back

1. An epistle for the self-sufficient, Romans contrasts the plight of people who choose to dress in self-made garments with those who gladly accept the robes of grace.

   A. What do you think Max means by "self-made garments"? Have you ever worn such "garments"? If so, explain.

   B. What do you think Max means by "the robes of grace"? Are these "robes" in your wardrobe? Explain.

2. God used the book of Romans to change the lives (and the wardrobes) of Luther, John Wesley, John Calvin, William Tyndale, St. Augustine, and millions of others. There is every reason to think he'll do the same for you.

   A. What comes to mind when you think of the book of Romans?

   B. What do you know of the men Max mentions in this paragraph—Luther, Wesley, Calvin, Tyndale, Augustine? How did Romans change their lives?

   C. How can the book of Romans change your own life? Do you think it will? Explain.

Looking Deep

1. Read Romans 1:16–17.

   A. How do these two verses explain the theme of Romans?

    B.   How does Paul use these verses to describe what he plans to unfold in the rest of his book?

    C.   Do you believe you have a good understanding of the topic described in these verses? Explain.

    D.   Are these verses being "lived out" in your daily life? Explain.

2. Read Galatians 3:26.

    A.   How does this verse compare to Romans 1:16–17?

    B.   What is common to each?

$\boxed{\text{I}}$

The Parable of the River

Looking Back

1. Though they did not know where they were, of one fact they were sure: They were not intended for this place.

   A. How did the sons know they were not intended for their new surroundings?

   B. In what way is this statement a description of our own circumstances?

2. One chose to indulge, the other to judge, and the third to work. None of them chose his father.

   A. With which of the three brothers are you most likely to identify? Explain.

   B. What is wrong with the responses of each of the three sons?

3. All four brothers heard the same invitation. Each had an opportunity to be carried home by the elder brother. The first said no, choosing a grass hut over his father's house. The second said no, preferring to analyze the mistakes of his brother rather than admit his own. The third said no, thinking it wiser to make a good impression than an honest confession. And the fourth said yes, choosing gratitude over guilt.

   A. What reasons did each of the three brothers give for refusing the offer of the eldest brother? Have you ever heard people give similar reasons for refusing Jesus' offer of salvation? If so, describe them.

B. How did the fourth brother choose "gratitude over guilt"?

4. As you read of the brothers, which describes your relationship to God? Have you, like the fourth son, recognized your helplessness to make the journey home alone? Do you take the extended hand of your father? Are you caught in the grip of his grace?

A. Answer the questions above.

B. How does someone know whether he or she is "caught in the grip of [God's] grace"?

5. What does Max mean by each of the following, and what do they all have in common?

A. The Hut-Building Hedonist

B. The Fault-Finding Judgmentalist

C. The Rock-Stacking Legalist

6. I might as well prepare you: The first chapters of Romans are not exactly upbeat. Paul gives us the bad news before he gives the good news. He will eventually tell us that we are all equal candidates for grace, but not before he proves that we are all desperately sinful.

A. Why do you think Paul began with the bad news before he explained the good news?

B. When we explain the gospel to someone, do we usually follow Paul's pattern? Explain.

Looking Deep

1. Read Ephesians 1:7–8

A. According to verse 7, what do we have in Christ?

B. According to what measure were we given these things, according to verses 7–8?

2. Read Ephesians 2:4–9

A. How are love, mercy and grace related to each other in verses 4–5? What do these three work together to achieve?

B. What future grace will we experience, according to verse 7?

C. What do you learn about grace in verses 8–9? How does this affect you personally?

$$\boxed{2}$$

God's Gracious Anger

Looking Back

1. God does not sit silently while his children indulge in perversion. He lets us go our sinful way and reap the consequences. Every broken heart, every unwanted child, every war and tragedy can be traced back to our rebellion against God.
   A. Why do you think God doesn't stop us before we "go our sinful way"?
   B. Do you agree that "every war and tragedy can be traced back to our rebellion against God"? Explain.

2. God is angry at evil. For many, this is a revelation.
   A. What does it mean that God is "angry" at evil?
   B. Was this a revelation to you? If so, explain.

3. Many don't understand God's anger because they confuse the wrath of God with the wrath of man. The two have little in common.
   A. How is the wrath of God different from the wrath of man?
   B. Do the two kinds of "wrath" have anything in common? If so, what?

4. Every star is an announcement. Each leaf a reminder. The glaciers are megaphones, the seasons are chapters, the clouds are banners. Nature is a song of many parts but one theme and one verse: *God is.*

    A.   How does nature proclaim that God exists?

    B.   If this is true, then why are there atheists?

5. The question is not, "How dare a loving God be angry?", but rather "How could a loving God feel anything less?"

    A.   Have you ever met someone who thought love and anger couldn't co-exist? If so, why did they believe this?

    B.   Why does Max believe that God must demonstrate both love and anger? Do you agree? Why or why not?

Looking Deep

1. Read Romans 1:18–20

    A.   Against whom is the "wrath of God" being revealed, according to verse 18? How is it being revealed?

    B.   Why is the "wrath of God" being revealed, according to verse 19?

    C.   Why are men "without excuse," according to verse 20?

2. Read Psalm 19:1–6

    A.   What do these verses teach us about God's creation?

    B.   What does God's creation teach us about God?

3

Godless Living

Looking Back

1. If there is no ultimate good behind the world, then how do we define "good" within the world? If the majority opinion determines good and evil, what happens when the majority is wrong?

   A.   How would you answer Max's two questions above?

   B.   Without God, can there be any truly "good" or "evil"? Explain.

2. What dike does the God-denying thinker have to stop the flood? What anchor will the secularist use to keep society from being sucked out to sea? If a society deletes God from the human equation, what sandbags will they stack against the swelling tide of barbarism and hedonism?

   A.   What kind of anchor is society's trust in?

   B.   What biblical examples of godlessness serve as wake-up calls for our society?

3. Mine deep enough in every heart and you'll find it: a longing for meaning, a quest for purpose. As surely as a child breathes, he will someday wonder, "What is the purpose of my life?"

   A.   Have you ever struggled with a longing for meaning or a sense of purpose? If so, describe the struggle. If not, why not?

   B.   What is the purpose of your life?

4. With God in your world, you aren't an accident nor an incident, you are a gift to the world, a divine work of art, signed by God.

    A.   Do you ever feel like an "accident" or an "incident"? If so, when are such feelings most likely to occur?

    B.   Do you believe you are a "gift to the world, a divine work of art, signed by God"? Explain.

5. Ironically, the more we know the less we worship. We are more impressed with our discovery of the light switch than with the one who invented electricity.

    A.   Do you agree that the more we know, the less we worship? Explain.

    B.   Why do you think it seems so easy to forget God?

6. According to Romans 1, godlessness is a bad swap. In living for today, the hut-building hedonist destroys his hope of living in a castle tomorrow.

    A.   How do people make this "bad swap" today?

    B.   Did you ever choose a "hut" over a "castle"? If so, describe the situation. What caused you to make a change?

Looking Deep

1. Read Romans 1:21–32.

    A.   What is the awful sin described in verse 21? What happens to those who commit such a sin?

    B.   What is the sin described in verses 22–23? How is this related to the sin of verse 21?

    C.   What is the sin described in verse 24? Does this seem related to the sin of verses 22–23? Explain.

    D.   How does verse 25 summarize verses 21–24?

    E.   Work through verses 26–32, noting how the passage intensifies as it progresses. What is the significance of this?

2. Read Ephesians 2:10.

    A.   How are believers described in this verse? What task are they given to do?

    B.   How firm is God in his intention for believers?

$$\boxed{4}$$

Godless Judging

Looking Back

1. Ever wrestled with the deathbed conversion of a rapist or the eleventh hour conversion of a child molester? We've sentenced them, maybe not in court, but in our hearts. We put them behind bars and locked the door. They are forever imprisoned by our disgust. And then, the impossible happens. They repent. Our response? (Dare we say it?) We cross our arms and furrow our brows, "God won't let you off that easy. Not after what you did. God is kind but he's no wimp. Grace is for average sinners like me, not deviants like you."

    A. What did you think when you read of Jeffrey Dahmer's reported conversion? Be honest.

    B. What would you say to a person who told you, "If your God could forgive Jeffrey Dahmer or Adolf Hitler, I want no part of him"?

2. It's one thing to be repulsed at the acts of a Jeffrey Dahmer (and I am). It's another entirely to claim that I am superior (I'm not), or that he is beyond the grace of God (no one is).

    A. What repulses us about the acts of a Jeffrey Dahmer? Why does one set of sins seem worse than another?

    B. Why is it so easy for us to believe we are superior to others?

    C. Why can Max say that no one is beyond the grace of God?

3. The easiest way to justify the mistakes in my house is to find worse ones in my neighbor's house.

A.   What does Max mean by the statement above?

B.   Do you agree with him? Why or why not?

4. The request Dahmer made is no different than yours or mine. He may make it from a prison bunk, you may make it from a church pew, but from heaven's angle we're all asking for the moon. And by heaven's grace we all receive it.

A.   Why was Dahmer's request no different than yours or mine?

B.   What does Max mean that "from heaven's angle we're all asking for the moon"?

Looking Deep

1. Read Romans 2:1–11.

A.   Why do those who pass judgment on others have no excuse? What are they actually doing when they pass judgment (verse 1)?

B.   What warning is given in verses 3–4?

C.   How can someone show "contempt" for God's kindness and patience, according to verse 5?

D.   Both a warning and a promise are given in verses 6–10. Describe each of them, and to whom each are given.

E.   What is the purpose of verse 11? Why is this important to say here?

2. Read Matthew 20:1–16.

A.   In a single sentence, what do you think the point of Jesus' parable is?

B.   What does he want us to know?

3. Read 1 Corinthians 4:5.

A.   What does this verse tell us *not* to do? What does it tell us to do?

B.   What does it say God will do? What does it say will be the result?

5

Godless Religion

Looking Back

1. Faith is intensely personal. There is no royal lineage or holy bloodline in God's kingdom.

    A. Why is faith "intensely personal"?

    B. What does Max mean that "there is no royal lineage or holy bloodline in God's kingdom"? Are you glad for this? Explain.

2. Paul is accusing the Jews of trusting the symbol of circumcision while neglecting their souls. Could he accuse us of the same error?

    A. How is it possible to trust a symbol while ignoring the spiritual reality the symbol represents?

    B. Answer Max's question above and explain your answer.

3. Symbols are important. Some of them, like communion and baptism, illustrate the cross of Christ. They symbolize salvation, demonstrate salvation, even articulate salvation. But they do not impart salvation.

    A. How do communion and baptism illustrate the cross of Christ?

    B. Why can't symbols impart salvation?

4. From God's perspective there is no difference between the ungodly partygoer, the ungodly finger-pointer, and the ungodly pew-sitter. The Penthouse gang, the courthouse clan, and the

church choir need the same message: Without God all are lost.

A. Why is there no difference between the three groups mentioned above?

B. What is the remedy for all three groups mentioned above?

5. There is only one name under heaven that has the power to save, and that name is not yours.

A. How is the modern world apt to respond to Max's statement above?

B. How would you respond to someone who objected to Max's statement?

Looking Deep

1. Read Romans 2:17–3:18.

A. What claims of superiority does Paul say Jews were making (2:17–20)?

B. What questions does Paul ask of the Jews (2:21–23)? What answers does he assume?

C. What is the connection of verse 24 to the preceding passage? In what way is this verse a conclusion?

D. What value does circumcision have, according to 2:25–29? What two kinds of people are contrasted?

E. What advantages does Paul say Jews have (3:1–4)?

F. What major problem is being discussed in 3:5–8? How would you answer the apostle's questions?

G. What major teaching is developed in 3:9–18? How does Paul do this? What does he conclude?

2. Read Acts 4:10–12.

A. How was the lame man healed according to verse 10?

B. How does Peter describe Jesus according to verses 10–11?

C. What claim does Peter make in verse 12? How is this significant?

6

Calling the Corpses

Looking Back

1. For all of our differences, there is one problem we all share. We are separated from God.

    A.   What does it mean to be "separated from God"?

    B.   What are some of the evidences that a person is separated from God?

    C.   How did we all come to be separated from God?

2. A dead flower has no life. A dead body has no life. A dead soul has no life. Cut off from God, the soul withers and dies. The consequence of sin is not a bad day or a bad mood, but a dead soul.

    A.   What does Max mean by "a dead soul"?

    B.   Why is the consequence of sin "a dead soul"?

3. We don't need more religion, we need a miracle. We don't need someone to disguise the dead, we need someone to raise the dead.

    A.   How is religion different from a miracle?

    B.   Who needs to be raised from the dead?

4. We are the corpse and he is the corpse-caller. We are the dead and he is the dead-raiser. Our task is not to get up but to admit we are dead. The only ones who remain in the grave are the ones who don't think they are there.

    A.   What does it mean to "admit we are dead"? What are the

consequences if we don't admit this?

B. How can someone not know they are "in the grave"? Do
    you know anyone like this? If so, explain.

Looking Deep

1. Read Romans 3:21–26.
    A. What two kinds of "righteousness" are contrasted in
        verses 21–22? What kind does God endorse?
    B. What does verse 23 tell us about ourselves? How is this
        significant?
    C. How does verse 24 solve the problem of verse 23?
    D. How do verses 25–26 explain how God can be perfectly
        just and yet declare us not guilty?
2. Read 2 Corinthians 5:17–18.
    A. What does it mean to be "in Christ"? How does one get
        to be "in Christ"?
    B. What is true of someone who is "in Christ"? Is this true
        of you? Explain.

7

Where Love and Justice Meet

Looking Back

1. What if, perish the thought, heaven had limitations to its coverage?

    A.   Answer Max's question above.

    B.   Do you know of anyone who believes heaven has "limitations to its coverage"? If so, describe what they believe these limitations to be.

2. It's one thing to make good people right, but those who are evil? We can expect God to justify the decent, but the dirty? Surely coverage is provided for the driver with the clean record, but the speeder? The ticketed? The high-risk client? How in the world can justification come for the evil?

    A.   In God's eyes, are there any "good people" (see Luke 18:19)? Any "decent" people? Any with a "clean record"? Explain.

    B.   How *can* justification come for the evil?

3. Salvation is God-given, God-driven, God-empowered, and God-originated. The gift is not from man to God. It is from God to man.

    A.   Why is it important to emphasize that salvation begins and ends with God?

    B.   Why is it important to remember that salvation is a gift?

4. Is God going to lower his standard so we can be forgiven? Is God going to look away and pretend that I've never sinned? Would we want a God who altered the rules and made exceptions?

    A.   What would be bad about God lowering his standard so we could be forgiven?

    B.   Would you want a God who altered the rules and made exceptions? Explain.

5. Ponder the achievement of God. He doesn't condone our sin, nor does he compromise his standard. He doesn't ignore our rebellion, nor does he relax his demands. Rather than dismiss our sin he assumes our sin and, incredibly, sentences himself. God's holiness is honored. Our sin is punished. And we are redeemed.

    A.   How did God "sentence himself"? What does this mean?

    B.   How does the cross both honor God's holiness and secure our redemption?

Looking Deep

1. Read Romans 4:4–8.

    A.   What two things are contrasted in verses 4 and 5? How are they different?

    B.   How does Paul use the words of David to support his contention in verse 5?

    C.   What does it mean to "trust God"? Is this a one-time event, or an ongoing action? Explain.

2. Read 2 Corinthians 5:19, 21.

    A.   What did God do, according to verse 19? How did he do this? What was the result?

    B.   What did God do, according to verse 21? Why did he do this? What was the result?

3. Read Colossians 2:13–15.
   A. How were we described in verse 13? How did God respond to this condition?
   B. How did God do this, according to verse 14?
   C. In what way does the cross show God's "triumph"? How is this possible?

8

Credit Where Credit Is Not Due

Looking Back

1. I don't always know the *occasion* of my sins. There are times when I sin and I don't even know it!

   A. How is it possible to sin and not be aware of it?

   B. Describe any instances you can think of in which you belatedly realized that you had committed some sin.

2. The cost of your sins is more than you can pay. The gift of your God is more than you can imagine.

   A. Suppose you only sinned once in your entire life. Could you pay that kind of debt? Explain.

   B. In what way is the gift of God more than we can imagine?

3. Grace is risky. There *is* the chance that people will take it to an extreme. There *is* the possibility that people will abuse God's goodness.

   A. Do you agree that "grace is risky"? Why or why not?

   B. In what ways have you seen that grace is risky? How have you seen people abuse God's goodness? Have you ever done so? Explain.

4. Grace fosters an eagerness for good. Grace doesn't spawn a desire to sin. If one has truly embraced God's gift, he will not mock it. In fact, if a person uses God's mercy as liberty to sin, one might wonder whether the person ever knew God's mercy at all.

A. Why does grace foster "an eagerness for good"? How does this work?

B. Do you agree with Max's last statement? Why or why not?

5. The vast majority of people simply state, "God may give grace to you, but not to me. You see, I've charted the waters of failure. I've pushed the envelope too many times. I'm not your typical sinner, I'm guilty of _____" and they fill in the blank.

A. Have you ever heard someone make a statement like that above? If so, describe what was said. How did you respond?

B. Do you ever feel as though you could make such a statement? How would you "fill in the blank"? What does God's Word say about this?

Looking Deep

1. Read Romans 4:13–24.

A. According to verse 13, how did Abraham receive God's promise? Why is this important (v. 14)?

B. Who may receive the benefits of the promise (vv. 16–17)?

C. Why is Abraham a particularly good example of a man who lived by faith (vv. 18–22)?

D. What part of Abraham's example do verses 23–24 encourage us to follow? Have you followed this example? Explain.

2. Read Galatians 3:2–14.

A. Paul asks at least five questions in Galatians 3:2–5. What are they, and what answer does the apostle expect for each?

B. What does Abraham illustrate in this passage (vv. 6–9)?

How does this compare to the Romans text above?

C.   How many people are justified through the law according to 3:10–12?

D.   How can we appropriate the promise to Abraham according to 3:13–14? What benefit does this bring?

$$\boxed{9}$$

Major League Grace

Looking Back

1. These guys didn't make it to the big leagues on skill, they made it on luck. They weren't picked because they were good, they were picked because they were willing.

   A. How does Max compare the striking ballplayers with the replacement players?

   B. Did the replacement players recognize their good fortune? How do we know?

2. If the first four chapters of Romans tell us anything, they tell us we are living a life we don't deserve. We aren't good enough to get picked, but look at us, suited up and ready to play!

   A. In what way are we "living a life we don't deserve"? How is this like the replacement ballplayers?

   B. How did we come to be "suited up and ready to play"? How did this happen? Who is responsible?

3. Peace with God. What a happy consequence of faith! Not just peace between countries, peace between neighbors, or peace at home; salvation brings peace with God.

   A. How would you describe "peace with God"? Of what does it consist?

   B. How is peace with God better than other kinds of peace?

4. Christ meets you outside the throne room, takes you by the

hand, and walks you into the presence of God. Upon entrance we find grace, not condemnation; mercy, not punishment.

A. Imagine yourself being led into the throne room of God by Jesus. How do you feel?

B. On what basis can we expect to find grace, not condemnation; and mercy, not punishment?

5. Because of God's grace we go from being people whose "throats are open graves" (v. 13) to being participants of God's glory. We were washed up and put out, now we are called up and put in.

A. In what ways are people whose "throats are open graves" different from those who are "participants in God's glory"?

B. In what way were we "washed up and put out"? In what way are we now "called up and put in"?

Looking Deep

1. Read Romans 5:1–3.

A. How are we "justified," according to 5:1? What does it mean to be "justified"? What result does this produce?

B. What does it mean to "stand" in "grace"? What result does this "standing" produce?

C. What two things don't seem to go together in 5:3? In what way does Paul put them together?

2. Read Isaiah 53:4–6.

A. What did Jesus do for us according to verse 4? What does this mean?

B. What happened to Jesus, according to verse 5? For what purpose did this happen?

C. How are we pictured in verse 6? What did the Lord do about this situation? Are you glad for this? Explain.

$$\boxed{10}$$

The Privilege of Paupers

Looking Back

1. Christ welcomes us to his table by virtue of his love and our request. It is not our offerings which grant us a place at the feast; indeed, anything we bring appears puny at his table. Our admission of hunger is the only demand.

    A. Why do our offerings appear puny at God's table? Why do we so often bring them anyway?

    B. What does Max mean by admitting our "hunger"? How do we do this? Have you done this? Explain.

2. God didn't look at our frazzled lives and say, "I'll die for you when you deserve it."

    A. Had God said such a thing, how would that affect you right now?

    B. Has anyone ever deserved for God to die for them? Explain.

3. Isn't there anyone who sees you for who you are and not what you did? Yes. There is one who does. Your king. When God speaks of you, he doesn't mention your plight, pain, or problem; he lets you share his glory. He calls you his child.

    A. Are you ever tempted to think of yourself by what you have done in life? What is wrong about such thinking?

    B. What does it mean to share God's glory? How does this affect you in practical terms?

4. Are you aware that the most repeated command from the lips of Jesus was, "Fear not"? Are you aware that the only phrase to appear in every book of the Bible is the one from heaven, "Don't be afraid?"

   A. How is it significant that Jesus' most common command was "fear not"? What does this assume?

   B. Why would God so often tell us not to be afraid? What is the best way to overcome such fear?

5. Consider the list of blessings at God's table found on pp. 104–105.

   A. Which of these blessings is most precious to you? Why?

   B. Which of these blessings seems most distant to you? Why?

   C. How can knowledge of these blessings practically affect the way you live?

Looking Deep

1. Read Romans 5:6–8.

   A. For whom did Christ die, according to verse 6? When did he die? Why did he die?

   B. What contrast does Paul play up in verses 7–8? By doing this, who and what does he wish to exalt? Explain.

2. Read Matthew 5:6.

   A. What group of people does Jesus describe in this verse? What promise does he give to them?

   B. Do you believe you are included in this group? Explain.

3. Read Psalm 103:8–18.

   A. List the characteristics of God described in this passage. How is each important to you personally?

   B. List the characteristics of human beings described in this passage. How does this list mesh with the first list?

| 11 |

Grace Works

Looking Back

1. How can we who have been made right not live righteous lives? How can we who have been loved, not love? How can we who have been blessed, not bless? How can we who have been given grace, not live graciously?

    A.   How would you answer Max's questions above?

    B.   In your own life, what are the greatest hindrances to living righteously, loving, blessing, and living graciously?

2. Perhaps we don't sin *so* God can give grace, but do we ever sin *knowing* God will give grace? Do we ever compromise tonight, knowing we'll confess tomorrow?

    A.   How would you answer Max's questions above?

    B.   What is wrong with compromising tonight if we know we'll confess tomorrow?

3. Christ has taken your place. There is no need for you to remain in the cell.

    A.   What "cell" is Max talking about?

    B.   What specific kinds of "cells" are you most likely to enter? Explain.

4. Baptism is a vow; a sacred vow of the believer to follow Christ. Just as a wedding celebrates the fusion of two hearts, baptism celebrates the union of sinner with Savior.

    A.   What parallels do you see between baptism and marriage? What differences are there?

B.   In what way does baptism celebrate the union of sinner with Savior? What kind of union is this?

5.   Before Christ our lives were out of control, sloppy, and indulgent. We didn't even know we were slobs until we met him. Then he moved in. Things began to change. Not overnight, but gradually. What we threw around we began putting away. What we neglected we cleaned up. What had been clutter became order.

A.   Did you know you were a "slob" before you met Christ? Explain.

B.   How have things changed in your own life since Christ moved in? Could an outsider notice the changes? Explain.

Looking Deep

1.   Read Romans 6:1–12.

A.   What is the problem Paul addresses in 6:1? Is this still a problem today? Explain.

B.   How does Paul answer his own question (vv. 2–4)?

C.   What truth does Paul lay out in verses 5–7? Is this truth helpful in a practical sense? Why or why not?

D.   What promise is given in verse 8? How does this connect with verse 11? What practical admonition does Paul then give in verse 12?

2.   Read Titus 2:11–12 (cf. 1:16).

A.   What has appeared "to all men"? What did this do (2:11)?

B.   What does grace teach us to do (2:12)? How does it do this?

C.   In what way is Titus 1:16 the flip side of 2:12?

3.   Read Acts 26:20.

A.   How does this verse reinforce the message of Titus 1:16 ?

B.   How does this verse reinforce the message of Titus 2:12?

12

Turning Yourself In

Looking Back

1. From the beginning God has called for honesty. He's never demanded perfection, but he has expected truthfulness.
    A. If God knows everything already, why would he demand honesty from us?
    B. If God knows everything already, why is it foolish not to be completely honest with him?

2. Confession does for the soul what preparing the land does for the field. Before the farmer sows the seed he works the acreage, removing the rocks and pulling the stumps. He knows that seed grows better if the land is prepared. Confession is the act of inviting God to walk the acreage of our hearts.
    A. In what ways is confession like a farmer preparing his land for crops?
    B. Is confession a regular practice of yours? Why or why not?

3. Confession seeks pardon from God, not amnesty. Pardon presumes guilt; amnesty, derived from the same Greek word as *amnesia*, "forgets" the alleged offense without imputing guilt. Confession admits wrong and seeks forgiveness; amnesty denies wrong and claims innocence.
    A. Why should we seek pardon, not amnesty? In your own words, what is the difference?
    B. How can we admit wrong and guilt without beginning to loathe ourselves?

4. Those who keep secrets from God, keep their distance from God. Those who are honest with God, draw near to God.

    A.   Is it really possible to keep secrets from God? Explain.

    B.   Why does honesty draw a person close to God?

5. May I ask a frank question? Are you keeping any secrets from God? Any parts of your life off limits? Any cellars boarded up or attics locked? Any part of your past or present that you hope you and God never discuss?

    A.   How would you answer Max's question above?

    B.   What areas of life are hardest for you to discuss with God? Why?

Looking Deep

1. Read Romans 6:18–23.

    A.   From what have believers been set free (v. 18)? To what have they become slaves?

    B.   What choice is laid out in verse 19? What choice are you making in this regard?

    C.   What question does Paul ask in verse 21? How would you answer him?

    D.   What contrast is made between verses 21 and 22?

    E.   What contrasts are made in verse 23? How are these crucial?

2. Read James 4:7–10.

    A.   What commands are given in this passage?

    B.   What promises are made in this passage?

    C.   In your own words, what is the main point of this passage?

3. Read James 5:16.

    A.   What does this verse instruct us to do? How often do we comply? Explain.

    B.   What promise is given here for those who do what they are instructed?

$$\boxed{13}$$

Sufficient Grace

Looking Back

1. There are times when the one thing you want is the one thing you never get.

    A. What one thing do you want that you've never received? How do you react to this?

2. When God says no to you, how will you respond? If God says, "I've given you my grace and that is enough," will you be content?

    A. Why do you think God sometimes tells us no?

    B. Are there any specific things you can do to be content with God's grace when he denies a request? If so, what are they?

3. Don't you find it encouraging that even Paul had a thorn in the flesh? There is comfort in learning that one of the writers of the Bible wasn't always on the same page with God.

    A. Do you find it encouraging that even Paul had a thorn in the flesh? Explain.

    B. Why does it help to remember that the writers of the Bible were real people with real problems?

4. You wonder why God doesn't remove temptation from your life? If he did, you might lean on your strength instead of his grace.

    A. What kind of temptations regularly give you the most difficulty? How do you deal with them?

B. In what areas are you tempted to lean on your own strength rather than his grace? When you do so, what is usually the result?

5. For all we don't know about thorns, we can be sure of this. God would prefer we have an occasional limp than a perpetual strut.

A. What "thorns" keep you from strutting?

B. Why is it better to "have an occasional limp than a perpetual strut"?

Looking Deep

1. Read 2 Corinthians 12:7–9.

A. Why was the "thorn" given to Paul (v. 7)? Who gave it to him? What was the "thorn's" task?

B. What was the apostle's response to the thorn (v. 8)?

C. What was God's response to Paul's request (v. 9)? How did Paul react to God's response? Do you think you would have reacted like this? Explain.

2. Read Philippians 4:6–7.

A. What should be our attitude toward anxiety, according to verse 6? How are we to respond to it? Is this usually your attitude? Explain.

B. What is the result of complying with the apostle's instruction of verse 6 (v. 7)? Have you experienced this result? Explain.

14

The Civil War of the Soul

Looking Back

1. You'd think that I would have no desire to use the alley, but I do! Part of me still wants the shortcut. Part of me wants to break the law.

    A. Have you ever felt the way Max said he does about the alley? If so, explain.

    B. Why do you think our struggle often intensifies when we hear that a desirable course of action is not allowed?

2. Those who have been amazed by grace have been equally amazed by their sin. Why do I say yes to God one day and yes to Satan the next?

    A. What amazes you about grace? What amazes you about your own sin?

    B. How would you answer Max's question above?

3. Are there weaknesses within you which stun you? Your words? Your thoughts? Your temper? Your greed? Your grudge? Your gossip? Things were better before you knew the law existed. But now you do. And now you have a war to wage.

    A. How would you answer Max's questions above?

    B. What internal war do you most often have to wage? Describe it.

4. Your temptation isn't late-breaking news in heaven. Your sin doesn't surprise God. He saw it coming. Is there any reason to

think that the one who received you the first time won't receive you every time?

   A.   Do you find it ironic that your sin surprises you, but not God? Explain.

   B.   How would you answer Max's question above?

5. What we consider shortcuts, God sees as disasters. He doesn't give laws for our pleasure. He gives them for our protection. In seasons of struggle we must trust his wisdom, not ours.

   A.   In what ways are God's laws for our protection? Do they exist for any other reason? Explain.

   B.   How can we practically learn to trust God's wisdom? How do you practice this habit? What tempts you away from it?

6. There is never a point in which you are any less saved than you were the first moment he saved you. Just because you were grumpy at breakfast doesn't mean you were condemned at breakfast. Your name doesn't disappear and reappear in the book of life according to your moods and actions. Such is the message of grace.

   A.   What do you think about Max's statements above? Do you agree with him? Why or why not?

   B.   If you *could* be condemned at breakfast because you were grumpy, what would that do to grace? What would "grace" mean in a world like that?

Looking Deep

1. Read Romans 7:7–25.

   A.   Is the law good or bad (vv. 7–12)? Yet what effect does the law have on us?

   B.   What is it that "kills" us (v. 13)?

   C.   What is Paul's struggle as described in verses 14–19? Do you see a similar struggle in yourself? If so, describe it.

D.   What conclusion does Paul make in verse 20? What is the significance of this conclusion?

E.   What general principle does Paul develop in verses 21–23? Is this principle at work in you? Explain.

F.   How does Paul respond to this general principle in verse 24? Can you identify with this reaction? Explain.

G.   Describe Paul's final reaction in verse 25. What is the reason for this joyful outburst?

2.   Read Romans 8:1.

A.   What does it mean to be in Christ Jesus?

B.   How does the truth of this verse change everything for us? Explain.

$\boxed{15}$

The Heaviness of Hatred

Looking Back

1. No one, I repeat *no one*, makes it through life free of injury. Someone, somewhere has hurt you. Part of you has died because someone spoke too much, demanded too much, or neglected too much.

   A. What have been the biggest "hurts" you've received through the years? How did you respond?

   B. What are the biggest hurts you've caused someone else? How did they respond?

2. Everyone gets wounded, hence everyone must decide: How many payments will I demand? We may not require that the offender write checks, but we have other ways of settling the score.

   A. What are some of the ways you've seen that people use to even the score?

   B. What are some of the ways you've used to try to even the score? How did these ways work out?

3. Keeping tabs on your mercy is not being merciful. If you're calibrating your grace, you're not being gracious. There should never be a point when our grace is exhausted.

   A. Why is it a contradiction to keep tabs on your mercy or calibrate your grace?

   B. What kinds of situations are most likely to exhaust your

grace? How do you deal with these situations?

4. To believe we are totally and eternally debt free is seldom easy. Even if we've stood before the throne and heard it from the king himself, we still doubt. As a result many are forgiven only a little, not because the grace of the king is limited, but because the faith of the sinner is small.

   A. Why isn't it easy to believe we are "totally and eternally debt free"?

   B. Have you been forgiven a little or a lot? Explain.

5. The longer we walk in the garden, the more likely we are to smell like flowers. The more we immerse ourselves in grace, the more likely we are to give grace.

   A. Who is the most gracious person you know? Describe him or her. What makes the person so gracious?

   B. How can we immerse ourselves in grace? What does that mean?

6. The key to forgiving others is to quit focusing on what they did to you and start focusing on what God did for you.

   A. What can you do to make it easier to quit focusing on what someone did to you?

   B. Take some time to make a list of the good things God did for you just this week. How many items are on your list?

Looking Deep

1. Read Romans 8:5–17.

   A. What two classes of people do verses 5–8 describe? Which one most describes you? Explain.

   B. How does Paul define a Christian in verse 9?

   C. What conclusion does Paul make in verses 10–11?

   D. Based on the conclusion he makes in verses 10–11, what kind of lifestyle does Paul say we should be living in verses 12–16?

E. What kind of future does Paul lay out for believers in verse 17? Should this make any difference in the way we live today? Explain.

2. Read Matthew 18:21–34.

A. How does the parable of verses 23–34 answer Peter's question in verse 21?

B. Have you ever failed to extend grace to another—one who owes you less than you owe Jesus?

3. Read Hebrews 12:15.

A. How is it possible to "miss" the grace of God, according to this verse?

B. What power does bitterness have, according to this verse? Why is it to be avoided? Are you avoiding it? Explain.

$$\boxed{16}$$

Life Aboard the Fellow-Ship

Looking Back

1. God has enlisted us in his navy and placed us on his ship. The boat has one purpose—to carry us safely to the other shore.

   A. Are you in God's navy? Are you aboard ship? How do you know?

   B. What part of the ship do you stay in?

2. We aren't called to a life of leisure, we are called to a life of service. Each of us has a different task.

   A. What is the specific task to which God has called you?

   B. How are you serving God on the "ship"?

3. Unity matters to God. The Father does not want his kids to squabble. Disunity disturbs him.

   A. As you honestly look at your own life, would you say you have more often helped to keep unity or to create disunity?

   B. Give an example of what you mean.

4. Nowhere, by the way, are we told to build unity. We are told simply to *keep* unity.

   A. What is the difference between "building" unity and "keeping" unity?

   B. How is this difference significant?

5. Unity doesn't begin in examining others, but in examining

self. Unity begins, not in demanding that others change, but in admitting that we aren't so perfect ourselves.

    A.   What kind of self-examination do you think Max is calling for here?

    B.   Reflect on personal examples and results of engaging in this kind of self-examination.

6. The answer to arguments? Acceptance. The first step to unity? Acceptance. Not agreement, acceptance. Not unanimity, acceptance.

    A.   What is the difference between acceptance and agreement?

    B.   What is the difference between acceptance and unanimity?

7. Just because a group is distributing toys at Christmas that doesn't mean they are Christians. Just because they are feeding the hungry that does not mean they are the honored ones of God. Jesus doesn't issue a call for blind tolerance.

    A.   Why is discernment an important part of unity?

    B.   What is the difference between acceptance and blind tolerance?

8. First, look at the fruit. Is it good? Is it healthy? Is he or she helping or hurting people? Production is more important than pedigree. The fruit is more important than the name of the orchard.

    A.   What does Max mean by "fruit" here?

    B.   What kind of "fruit" are you producing? Would others agree? Explain.

9. Also look at the faith. In whose name is the work done? Jesus was accepting of this man's work because it was done in the name of Christ.

    A.   Should we judge someone's faith? If so, what does this mean and how can it be done?

    B.   Just because someone uses the name "Jesus," does that mean they believe in the Jesus of the Bible?

10. Where there is faith, repentance, and a new birth, there is a Christian. When I meet a man whose faith is in the cross and eyes are on the Savior, I meet a brother.

    A.   Does Max's statement above make you pleased or uncomfortable?

    B.   Explain your answer.

Looking Deep

1. Read Romans 14:1–13.

    A.   What is the main topic of this passage? Give evidence to support your belief.

    B.   What examples does Paul give to illustrate his main point? List them.

    C.   Consider Paul's questions in verses 4 and 10. How do these questions relate to Paul's main point?

    D.   How do verses 11–12 add strength to Paul's instruction?

    E.   What conclusion does Paul make in verse 13? Why do you think the apostle spends so much time on this topic?

2. Read Ephesians 4:3–7.

    A.   What command is given in verse 3? How is this to be accomplished?

    B.   What reason for this command is given in verses 4–6?

    C.   How does verse 7 explain the power to fulfill this command?

17

What We Really Want to Know

Looking Back

1. There is no way our little minds can comprehend the love of God. But that didn't keep him from coming.

   A. Do you understand God's love better today than you did five years ago? Explain.

   B. Why is it good news that God's love is beyond our full comprehension?

2. God is with you. Knowing that, who is against you? Can death harm you now? Can disease rob your life? Can your purpose be taken or your value diminished? No. Though hell itself may set itself against you, no one can defeat you. You are protected. God is with you.

   A. When are you most likely to fear that God is *not* with you? How do you respond to these instances?

   B. Answer Max's questions above. Why do you give these answers?

3. Did God save you so you would fret? Would he teach you to walk just to watch you fall? Would he be nailed to the cross for your sins and then disregard your prayers?

   A. Answer Max's questions above.

   B. What is the point of asking the questions above?

4. Satan cannot accuse you. No one can accuse you! Fingers may point and voices may demand, but the charges glance off like

arrows hitting a shield. No more dirty dishwater. No more penance. No more nagging sisters. You have stood before the judge and heard him declare, "Not guilty."

A.   Why is Satan unable to make accusations against you that stick?

B.   How could we have been declared "not guilty" by the judge?

5.   "You wonder how long my love will last? Find your answer on a splintered cross, on a craggy hill. That's me you see up there, your maker, your God, nail-stabbed and bleeding. Covered in spit and sin-soaked. That's your sin I'm feeling. That's your death I'm dying. That's your resurrection I'm living. That's how much I love you."

A.   Why is the cross God's final answer to how much he loves us?

B.   How does the cross guarantee that God will always see to our welfare despite whatever hardships we may face?

Looking Deep

1.   Read Romans 8:31–39.

A.   What is Paul's question in verse 31? What does he intend to suggest by asking this question?

B.   Explain the apostle's logic behind his statement in verse 32. Why is this statement so crucial to daily living?

C.   In what way are the questions of verses 33–35 related? What is their function?

D.   How can the quotation found in verse 36 actually be an encouragement? How is it intended to function in this way?

E.   What is the connection of verse 37 to verse 36? What is the apostle's point?

F.   Does Paul leave anything out of verses 38–39? What does he intend for us to understand? How does he want these truths to encourage us?

2. Read Isaiah 49:15–16.

A. What question is asked in verse 15? What answer is expected? What comparison is intended with the subsequent statement?

B. What metaphor does God use in verse 16? What is his point? What does he want us to believe? Why?

3. Read Isaiah 50:7–10.

A. What attitude does the writer adopt in verse 10? Why?

B. How do verses 8–9 foreshadow Paul's words in Romans 8:31–39?

C. Who is addressed in verse 10? What instruction is given? Do you follow this instruction? Explain.

Conclusion

"Don't Forget About Me"

Looking Back

1. Unashamed of his needs, Billy Jack didn't let a flight attendant pass without a reminder: "Don't forget to look after me." I honestly can't think of one time Billy Jack didn't remind the crew that he needed attention. The rest of us didn't. We never asked for help. We were grown-up. Sophisticated. Self-reliant.

    A. In what way can Billy Jack be a good example for us?

    B. Why didn't the rest of the people on this flight ask the crew for extra attention? In what way is this similar to those who refuse to ask God for help?

2. Midway through the writing of this book I remembered Billy Jack. He would have understood the idea of grace. He knew what it was like to place himself totally in the care of someone else.

    A. Why does Max think Billy Jack would have understood the idea of grace?

    B. How do you think Billy Jack might define grace?

3. It occurred to me that Billy Jack was the safest person on the flight. Had the plane encountered trouble, he would have received primary assistance. The flight attendants would have bypassed me and gone to him. Why? He had placed himself in the care of someone stronger.

A.   Why would Billy Jack have been the safest person on the flight?

B.   Have you placed yourself in the care of someone stronger? Explain.

4.   One thing's for sure: You cannot save yourself. The river is too strong, the distance is too great. God has sent his firstborn son to carry you home. Are you firmly in the grip of his grace?

A.   Why can't we save ourselves?

B.   Answer Max's question above: Are you firmly in the grip of God's grace? How do you know?

Looking Deep

1.   Read Romans 10:1–13.

A.   What error did Paul say his countrymen made in verses 1–3?

B.   How is verse 4 the answer to this error?

C.   What two methods of justification are contrasted in verses 5–8? How does each work? Have you opted for either one? If so, which? Why?

D.   According to verses 9–10, how is one saved? Have you done this? Explain.

E.   What promise is given in verse 11? Why is this important?

F.   What summary statement is made in verses 12–13? In what way does this sum up the message of *In The Grip Of Grace*? How?

2.   Read Romans 11:33–36.

A.   What prompted these verses of glowing praise? What got Paul so excited?

B.   Does this excite you as well? Explain.

IMAGINE STUDYING THE BIBLE WITH
MAX LUCADO

The *Inspirational Study Bible*, edited by Max Lucado, includes:

- 700 "Life Lessons" from Lucado and other Christian authors
- 48 Color Pages address topics from Forgiveness to Victory
- Dramatic, Colorful Book Introductions by Max Lucado
- Two popular translations: New Century Version and the New King James Version
- Dictionary/Concordance
- Topical Index

"Stories of real people, real problems, real joy, and a real Savior."

Max Lucado, *General Editor*

The First Study Bible for the Heart

JOHN

INTRODUCTION

He's an old man, this one who sits on the stool and leans against the wall. Eyes closed and face soft, were it not for his hand stroking his beard, you'd think he was asleep.

Some in the room assume he is. He does this often during worship. As the people sing, his eyes will close and his chin will fall until it rests on his chest, and there he will remain motionless. Silent.

Those who know him well know better. They know he is not resting. He is traveling. Atop the music he journeys back, back, back until he is young again. Strong again. There again. There on the seashore with James and the apostles. There on the trail with the disciples and the women. There in the Temple with Caiaphas and the accusers.

It's been sixty years, but John sees him still. The decades took John's strength, but they didn't take his memory. The years dulled his sight, but they didn't dull his vision. The seasons may have wrinkled his face, but they didn't soften his love.

He had been with God. God had been with him. How could he forget?

❧ The wine that moments before had been water—John could still taste it.

❧ The mud placed on the eyes of the blind man in Jerusalem—John could still remember it.

❧ The aroma of Mary's perfume as it filled the room—John could still smell it.

And the voice. Oh, the voice. His voice. John could still hear it.

I am the light of the world, it rang... I am the door... I am the way, the truth, the life.

I will come back, it promised, and take you to be with me.

Those who believe in me, it assured, will have life even if they die.

John could hear him. John could see him. Scenes branded on his heart. Words seared into his soul. John would never forget. How could he? He had been there.

He opens his eyes and blinks. The singing has stopped. The teaching has begun. John looks at the listeners and listens to the teacher.

If only you could have been there, he thinks.

But he wasn't. Most weren't. Most weren't even born. And most who were there are dead. Peter is. So is James. Nathanael, Martha, Philip. They are all gone. Even Paul, the apostle who came late, is dead.

Only John remains.

He looks again at the church. Small but earnest. They lean forward to hear the teacher. John listens to him. What a task. Speaking of one he never saw. Explaining words he never heard. John is there if the teacher needs him.

But what will happen when John is gone? What will the teacher do then? When John's voice is silent and his tongue stilled? Who will tell them how Jesus silenced the waves? Will they hear how he fed the thousands? Will they remember how he prayed for unity?

How will they know? If only they could have been there.

Suddenly, in his heart he knows what to do.

Later, under the light of a sunlit shaft, the old fisherman unfolds the scroll and begins to write the story of his life...

In the beginning there was the Word...

LIFE LESSON
John 1:1-51

SITUATION 🖉 The Greeks and the Jews were familiar with the concept of the *word*. For the Jews it was an expression of God's wisdom, and for the Greeks it meant reason and intellect.

OBSERVATION 🖉 Leaving his heavenly home, Jesus put on human flesh to bring us God's Good News.

INSPIRATION 🖉 It all happened in a moment, a most remarkable moment.... that was like none other. For through that segment of time a spectacular thing occurred. God became a man. While the creatures of earth walked unaware, Divinity arrived. Heaven opened herself and placed her most precious one in a human womb....

God as a fetus. Holiness sleeping in a womb. The creator of life being created.

God was given eyebrows, elbows, two kidneys, and a spleen. He stretched against the walls and floated in the amniotic fluids of his mother.

God had come near....

The hands that first held him were unmanicured, calloused, and dirty.

No silk. No ivory. No hype. No party. No hoopla.

Were it not for the shepherds, there would have been no reception. And were it not for a group of star-gazers, there would have been no gifts....

Christ Comes to the World

*I*n the beginning there was the Word.[n] The Word was with God, and the Word was God. [2]He was with God in the beginning. [3]All things were made by him, and nothing was made without him. [4]In him there was life, and that life was the light of all people. [5]The Light shines in the darkness, and the darkness has not overpowered it.

[6]There was a man named John[n] who was sent by God. [7]He came to tell people the truth about the Light so that through him all people could hear about the Light and believe. [8]John was not the Light, but he came to tell people the truth about the Light. [9]The true Light that gives light to all was coming into the world!

[10]The Word was in the world, and the world was made by him, but the world did not know him. [11]He came to the world that was his own, but his own people did not accept him. [12]But to all who did accept him and believe in him he gave the right to become children of God. [13]They did not become his children in any human way—by any human parents or human desire. They were born of God.

[14]The Word became a human and lived among us. We saw his glory—the glory that belongs to the only Son of the Father—and he was full of grace and truth. [15]John tells the truth about him and cries out, saying, "This is the One I told you about: 'The One who comes after me is greater than I am, because he was living before me.'"

[16]Because he was full of grace and truth, from him we all received one gift after another. [17]The law was given through Moses, but grace and truth came through Jesus Christ. [18]No one has ever seen God. But God the only Son is very close to the Father,[n] and he has shown us what God is like.

John Tells People About Jesus

[19]Here is the truth John[n] told when the Jews in Jerusalem sent priests and Levites to ask him, "Who are you?"

[20]John spoke freely and did not refuse to answer. He said, "I am not the Christ."

[21]So they asked him, "Then who are you? Are you Elijah?"[n]

He answered, "No, I am not."

"Are you the Prophet?"[n] they asked.

He answered, "No."

[22]Then they said, "Who are you? Give us an answer to tell those who sent us. What do you say about yourself?"

[23]John told them in the words of the prophet Isaiah:
"I am the voice of one
  calling out in the desert:
'Make the road straight for the Lord.'"
Isaiah 40:3

Word The Greek word is "logos," meaning any kind of communication; it could be translated "message." Here, it means Christ, because Christ was the way God told people about himself.
John John the Baptist, who preached to people about Christ's coming (Matthew 3, Luke 3).
But...Father This could be translated, "But the only God is very close to the Father." Also, some Greek copies say, "But the only Son is very close to the Father."
John John the Baptist, who preached to people about Christ's coming (Matthew 3, Luke 3).
Elijah A man who spoke for God. He lived hundreds of years before Christ and was expected to return before Christ (Malachi 4:5-6).
Prophet They probably meant the prophet that God told Moses he would send (Deuteronomy 18:15-19).

24Some Pharisees who had been sent asked John: 25"If you are not the Christ or Elijah or the Prophet, why do you baptize people?"

26John answered, "I baptize with water, but there is one here with you that you don't know about. 27He is the One who comes after me. I am not good enough to untie the strings of his sandals."

28This all happened at Bethany on the other side of the Jordan River, where John was baptizing people.

29The next day John saw Jesus coming toward him. John said, "Look, the Lamb of God,*n* who takes away the sin of the world! 30This is the One I was talking about when I said, 'A man will come after me, but he is greater than I am, because he was living before me.' 31Even I did not know who he was, although I came baptizing with water so that the people of Israel would know who he is."

32-33Then John said, "I saw the Spirit come down from heaven in the form of a dove and rest on him. Until then I did not know who the Christ was. But the God who sent me to baptize with water told me, 'You will see the Spirit come down and rest on a man; he is the One who will baptize with the Holy Spirit.' 34I have seen this happen, and I tell you the truth: This man is the Son of God."

The First Followers of Jesus

35The next day John*n* was there again with two of his followers. 36When he saw Jesus walking by, he said, "Look, the Lamb of God!"*n*

37The two followers heard John say this, so they followed Jesus. 38When Jesus turned and saw them following him, he asked, "What are you looking for?"

They said, "Rabbi, where are you staying?" ("Rabbi" means "Teacher.")

39He answered, "Come and see." So the two men went with Jesus and saw where he was staying and stayed there with him that day. It was about four o'clock in the afternoon.

40One of the two men who followed Jesus after they heard John speak about him was Andrew, Simon Peter's brother. 41The first thing Andrew did was to find his brother Simon and say to him, "We have found the Messiah." ("Messiah" means "Christ.")

42Then Andrew took Simon to Jesus. Jesus looked at him and said, "You are Simon son of John. You will be called Cephas." ("Cephas" means "Peter."*n*)

43The next day Jesus decided to go to Galilee. He found Philip and said to him, "Follow me."

44Philip was from the town of Bethsaida, where Andrew and Peter lived. 45Philip found Nathanael and told him, "We have found the man that Moses wrote about in the law, and the prophets also wrote about him. He is Jesus, the son of Joseph, from Nazareth."

46But Nathanael said to Philip, "Can anything good come from Nazareth?"

Philip answered, "Come and see."

47As Jesus saw Nathanael coming toward him, he said, "Here is truly an Israelite. There is nothing false in him."

For thirty-three years he would feel everything you and I have ever felt. He felt weak. He grew weary. He was afraid of failure. He was susceptible to wooing women. He got colds, burped, and had body odor. His feelings got hurt. His feet got tired. And his head ached.

To think of Jesus in such a light is—well, it seems almost irreverent, doesn't it? It's not something we like to do; it's uncomfortable. It is much easier to keep the humanity out of the incarnation. He's easier to stomach that way. . . .

But don't do it. For heaven's sake, don't. Let him be as human as he intended to be. Let him into the mire and muck of our world. For only if we let him in can he pull us out.

(From *God Came Near* by Max Lucado)

APPLICATION If people want to know what God is like, they can look at Jesus. If they want to know what Jesus is like, they should be able to look at his followers. Can people see Christ in you?

EXPLORATION The Word is Born—John 14:6-7; 1 Corinthians 8:5-6; Galatians 4:4; Philippians 2:7, 8; 1 Timothy 3:16; Hebrews 2:14; 13:8; 1 John 1:1-2; 4:2.

Lamb of God Name for Jesus. Jesus is like the lambs that were offered for a sacrifice to God.
Peter The Greek name "Peter," like the Aramaic name "Cephas," means "rock."

MAX LUCADO can be heard daily on the radio program
UpWords. For information, write:

> *UpWords*
> P.O. Box 692170
> San Antonio, Texas 78269
>
> or call 1-800-822-9673